Getting Started in Jewish Genealogy
2016–2017 Edition

by Gary Mokotoff

Avotaynu

New Haven, CT
2016

Avotaynu, Inc.
794 Edgewood Ave.
New Haven, CT 06515

Printed in the United States of America

Front cover illustration, "A Family Tree of the Jewish People," by Caroline Guillot

Library of Congress Cataloging-in-Publication Data

Names: Mokotoff, Gary, author.
Title: Getting started in Jewish genealogy / by Gary Mokotoff.
Description: 2016-2017 edition. | New Haven, CT : Avotaynu, 2016. | Includes index.
Identifiers: LCCN 2016042023 | ISBN 9780983697596 (alk. paper)
Subjects: LCSH: Jews—Genealogy—Handbooks, manuals, etc.
Classification: LCC CS21 .M65 2016 | DDC 929.1072--dc23 LC record available at https://lccn.loc.gov/2016042023

To my wife, Ruth

My closest advisor, critic and confidant

Contents

Introduction

This book is not a beginner's guide. A beginner's guide to Jewish genealogy would undoubtedly require many more pages. It is a getting started guide; a guide meant to convince the reader that tracing one's Jewish ancestry can be done.

There is a wealth of resources available for family history research.[1] It is virtually impossible for a person to have lived on this Earth without leaving some documents of his/her existence. Our ancestors were born, married, died, were buried, emigrated, immigrated, were counted in censuses, did military service, attended school, bought property and/or did something newsworthy. Each of these events created documents. The purpose of this book is to make the reader aware of how to locate these documents and what they might contain.

The resources described are primarily Internet resources. The Internet has revolutionized family history research. What once took days or months now takes minutes or hours. When I started tracing the Mokotoff family history in the early 1980s, I acquired the Ellis Island (passenger arrival) record of my ancestors by traveling 31 miles to the local branch of the U.S. National Archives. Upon arrival, I searched an index on microfilm that provided information about when they arrived. A second microfilm had the actual passenger manifest which had to be brought to a microfilm printer at the facility to make a hard copy of the record. It was a half-day effort that necessitating payment for tolls and fuel. Today, I go to Ancestry.com on the Internet, key in the name of the ancestor and, within a minute or two, I can bring up the passenger manifest and print the document on my computer's printer. Total cost is a subscription to Ancestry.com. In the case of Ellis Island passenger records, there is an Internet resource where you can acquire the records at no cost. It is described elsewhere in this book.

This book ends with a case study. It shows how I was able to trace the paternal ancestry of the notorious Bernie Madoff back five generations—200 years—to 1809. The whole process took less than two hours (and 30 years of acquired skills). It used Internet resources such as Google; census, naturalization and immigration records; and a remarkable Internet site called JewishGen. Nearly half of the time was spent solving the problem that Madoff was not the name in the Old Country. Even that brick wall was overcome using the two most important attributes of a family historian: persistence and patience.

All reference works suffer from the fact that they are obsolete the day they are published. This is certainly true of books such as this one, because new resources are made available regularly, Internet sites shift to new locations, and existing

---

[1] "Family history" is the new politically correct term for "genealogy."

resources are modified or improved. It is the intent of the author to publish a new version of this book every year, hence the inclusion in the title of "2016–2017 Edition." This is made possible because of a new printing technology called Print On Demand. No longer must publishers guess how many books can be sold and order the estimated quantity. Now books can be printed as needed. This eliminates the motive to delay revised editions of a book.

The author would like to thank people who vetted portions of this book. Warren Blatt, managing director of JewishGen, checked the chapter on his organization. Stephen P. Morse read the chapter about his One-Step website. Eileen Polakoff provided advice on the overall book. Finally my wife, Ruth, converted my almost English into correct grammar and style.

Gary Mokotoff
New Haven, CT
September 2016

If I Can Do It, So Can You

As the author of this book, I would like to introduce myself to you, genealogically speaking.

My name is Gary Mokotoff. I was born in New York in 1937.

My father's name was Jack Mokotoff. He was born in New York in 1914 and died there in 1982.

His father's name was Morris Mokotoff. He was born in a small town about 30 miles south of Warsaw, Poland, called Warka. He came to the United States in 1911 (I have the ship's manifest) and died in Brooklyn in 1946.

That is all I knew about the Mokotoff family history until I became involved in family history research. I now can go back five more generations.

My great-grandfather's name was Hyman Mokotoff. He was born as Chaim Meir Mokotów in Siedlce, Poland, on September 27, 1851, and died in New York (Manhattan) on February 18, 1921. He married his first cousin, Gussie (Gitla) Mokotów, in Warka, on August 28, 1874. I know these dates because I have Hyman's birth, marriage and death records.

His father, my great-great-grandfather, was Menachem Mendel Mokotów. He was born about 1819 in Warka, Poland, and died between 1874 and 1877, perhaps not in Warka. I don't have his birth record, but I know his approximate year of birth from the birth records of his children, where he had to give his age at the time of each child's birth. I know he died no earlier than 1874, because his son Hyman's marriage record shows that he was living at the time of Hyman's marriage. He died no later than 1877, because the first son of Hyman and Gussie Mokotów was born that year and was named Menachem Mendel, after his grandfather. Ashkenazic Jews—the Jews whose origins are Central and Eastern Europe—name their children after deceased relatives, so Menachem Mendel (senior) had to have been deceased by the time Menachem Mendel (junior), his grandson, was born.

Menachem Mendel's father's name—my great-great-great-grandfather—was Tuvia David Mokotów (Tobiasz Dawid in Polish). He was born about 1774 (based on the birth records of his children where he had to give his age) and died in Warsaw, Poland, on January 18, 1842 (from his death record).

His father—my great-great-great-great grandfather—was named Moshe ben Aron (Moses, son of Aron—Mosiek Aronowicz in Polish), that is, he never had a last name. One of the rewarding aspects of tracing your ancestry is that you learn a lot about history, especially Jewish history. You learn that before the beginning of the 19th century, most Jews of Central and Eastern Europe did not have hereditary surnames (last names). At that time, the three great superpowers—the German Empire, the Russian Empire and the Austro-Hungarian Empire—independently enacted laws requiring Jews to acquire hereditary surnames, that is fixed last names that would be passed down from a father to his sons. So if your name is Goldstein, Aronowitz, Schneider or Warshawsky, your name is only 200 years old.

There is a myth that when Jews acquired hereditary surnames, they had to pay a bribe to Christian authorities to avoid getting derogatory ones. In reality, in most of Central and Eastern Europe, it was the Jewish community that was given the responsibility of assigning surnames.[2] It is likely that many Jews converted their nicknames to hereditary surnames. Even a small *shtetl* (Yiddish for "village") like Warka undoubtedly had a number of men named Moshe, so the man known as "Moshe the tailor" (Moshe der Schneider, in Yiddish) became (in Polish) Mosiek Sznajder. "Moshe from Warsaw" became Mosiek Warszawski—the *ski* ending meaning "of" (Warsaw). The old man named Moshe didn't want to be bothered with this government edict, so not having acquired a surname, he was given the surname Aronowicz, which merely means "son of Aron." The second "Moshe the tailor" in town could not be called Schneider also, so he might have selected a pretty name such as Goldstein (gold stone) because it had the connotation that he was a rich man, which he was not.

As to the surname Mokotów, my great-great-great-grandfather, Tuvia, chose a town name, Mokotów, which was a small village just south of Warsaw and about 30 miles (50 km) north of Warka, where he lived. As Warsaw grew, it absorbed the village of Mokotów, and today it is the southern section of the capital of Poland. Does it mean that the ancestral town of the Mokotoff family is not Warka, but Mokotów? I can find no evidence that Tuvia came from Mokotów or even that Jews lived in the town at the beginning of the 19th century. There is a family legend that Tuvia took the name Mokotów because he liked the way it sounded. "Mokotów" has the phonetic association with *m' kitov*, which in Hebrew means "for He is good." *Tov* also was the root of his given name, Tuvia, which means "for the good of God."

Returning to the Mokotoff/Mokotów ancestry, as noted above, my great-great-great-great grandfather was Moshe ben Aron (Moses, son of Aron). He died on July 25, 1810, at the age of 83. How do I know the exact date? Because I have his death record (see illustration on next page). How do I know he is related to me? Because the death record states on line 11 that Dawid Mokotów was his son (*Dawida Mokotówa Syna*). As noted above, when I started tracing my Mokotów family history, I only knew the names of my father and grandfather. Today, I can take my family history back four more generations to a man named Moshe ben

[2] Exception was the Austro-Hungarian Empire which included Galicia. Consult *A Dictionary of Jewish Surnames from the Russian Empire: Revised Edition,* by Alexander Beider. Bergenfield, NJ: Avotaynu, 2008.

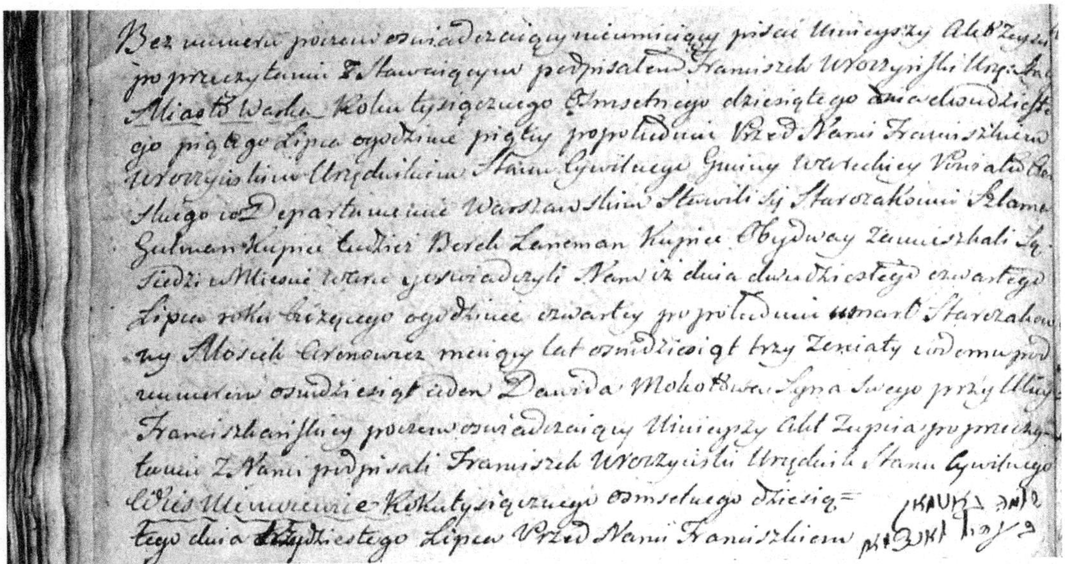

Death record of Mosiek Aronowicz from the 1810 vital records register of Warka, Poland. At the end of line 9 it states "umarł Starozakonnay Mosiek Aronowicz" (died the Jew Moses son of Aron). On line 11, it states "Dawida Mokotówa Syna" (David Mokotów, son).

Aron who was born about 1727. In fact, it could be argued that my family history goes back one more generation, possibly to the late 1600s, to a man named Aron ben ?. The purpose of this book is to demonstrate that if I can trace my ancestry back eight generations to a man named Aron ben Question Mark, there is a strong likelihood that so can you.

Four Myths of Jewish Genealogy

There are four great myths of Jewish genealogy:

• Nobody remembers. All persons interviewed say they know nothing about the family's history. Personal experience indicates that this is not true. You have to ask the right questions.

• All the records were destroyed in the Holocaust. While it is true that most things Jewish were destroyed in the Holocaust, family history research is primarily about locating records of your ancestors, and these records are invariably government records, not Jewish records.

• My family name was changed ("at Ellis Island") and no one knows the original name. While this is an obstacle, there are ways of determining the original name. They are discussed in this book.

• No one knows what town we came from. This too is an obstacle, but how it can be overcome is also discussed in this book.

Get Started by Interviewing People

I began tracing the Mokotoff family history by approaching my father and asking him what he knew about the Mokotoffs. His answer was, "Nothing." It was not true. In reality my father knew a lot. I had asked the wrong question. I should have asked him such questions as:

• Do you have any documents about your parents or other members of the family?

• Do you have old photos of the family? Please identify the people in the pictures, the occasion and the date.

• Do you know the dates and places of life events—births, marriages and deaths of members of the family?

• Who are you named after? Jews usually name their children after deceased relatives. The answer to the question may add another ancestor to the family tree.

Unfortunately, all these questions were not asked in my father's lifetime; instead I had to rely on his memorabilia which I examined after his death.

Ask for Documents

My father had a number of documents pertaining to his parents. He had their wedding announcement which gave me the exact date of their marriage. His parents were divorced. He had a copy of their *get* (Jewish divorce papers). The most interesting document he had was his mother's application for derivative citizenship; that is, his mother was claiming the right to be declared a U.S. citizen derived from the fact that her husband, my grandfather, was a naturalized citizen. Governments love to ask lots of questions of their soon-to-be citizens, and this form had a wealth of information. The information on the document provided:

• Date and place of birth of my grandmother as she informed the government

• Her mother's maiden name—the only document in my possession with this information

• The date and name of the ship on which she arrived in the U.S.

There are many documents in the possession of your family members that might be of value: announcements of family events (birth, bar/bat mitzvah, engagement, marriage, death), passports, union cards, naturalization certificates, newspaper clippings, military discharge papers, correspondence—any document that provides a historical record of the family. Ask members of the family what documents they have that will assist in determining the family's history.

Ask for Photos

Whenever I asked my mother when her parents were married, she would say, "I don't know." Whenever I showed my mother a photo of her family that included her parents and all their then-living descendants, she remarked, "Oh, that is a picture of my parents' 35th wedding anniversary. I was pregnant with you at

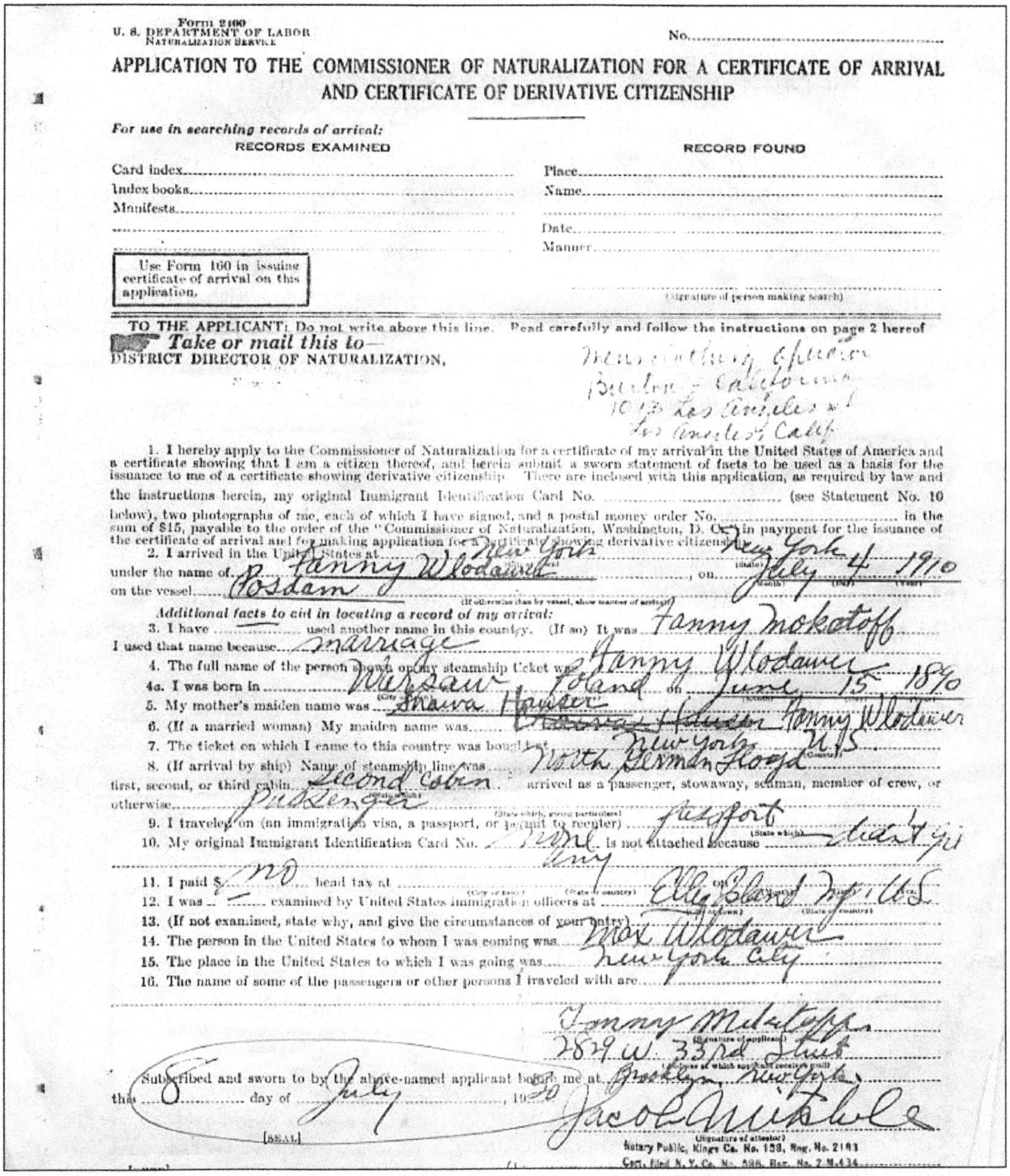

Form 2400
U. S. DEPARTMENT OF LABOR
NATURALIZATION SERVICE

No. ....

APPLICATION TO THE COMMISSIONER OF NATURALIZATION FOR A CERTIFICATE OF ARRIVAL AND CERTIFICATE OF DERIVATIVE CITIZENSHIP

For use in searching records of arrival:

RECORDS EXAMINED	RECORD FOUND
Card index..........	Place..........
Index books..........	Name..........
Manifests..........	....
....	Date..........
....	Manner..........

Use Form 160 in issuing certificate of arrival on this application.

(Signature of person making search)

TO THE APPLICANT: Do not write above this line. Read carefully and follow the instructions on page 2 hereof

Take or mail this to—
DISTRICT DIRECTOR OF NATURALIZATION, Naturalization Officer Bureau California 1013 Los Angeles ... Los Angeles Calif

1. I hereby apply to the Commissioner of Naturalization for a certificate of my arrival in the United States of America and a certificate showing that I am a citizen thereof, and herein submit a sworn statement of facts to be used as a basis for the issuance to me of a certificate showing derivative citizenship. There are inclosed with this application, as required by law and the instructions herein, my original Immigrant Identification Card No. .... (see Statement No. 10 below), two photographs of me, each of which I have signed, and a postal money order No. .... in the sum of $15, payable to the order of the "Commissioner of Naturalization, Washington, D. C." in payment for the issuance of the certificate of arrival and for making application for a certificate showing derivative citizenship.

2. I arrived in the United States at New York New York under the name of Fanny Wlodawer on July 4 1910 on the vessel Posdam

Additional facts to aid in locating a record of my arrival:

3. I have —— used another name in this country. (If so) It was Fanny Mokotoff
I used that name because marriage
4. The full name of the person shown on my steamship ticket was Fanny Wlodawer
4a. I was born in Warsaw Poland on June 15 1890
5. My mother's maiden name was Shawa Hauser
6. (If a married woman) My maiden name was ~~Shawa Hauser~~ Fanny Wlodawer
7. The ticket on which I came to this country was bought at New York U.S.
8. (If arrival by ship) Name of steamship line was North German Lloyd first, second, or third cabin Second Cabin arrived as a passenger, stowaway, seaman, member of crew, or otherwise passenger
9. I traveled on (an immigration visa, a passport, or permit to reenter) passport
10. My original Immigrant Identification Card No. none is not attached because ....
11. I paid $ no head tax at ....
12. I was — examined by United States immigration officers at Ellis Island N.Y. U.S.
13. (If not examined, state why, and give the circumstances of your entry) ....
14. The person in the United States to whom I was coming was Max Wlodawer
15. The place in the United States to which I was going was New York City
16. The name of some of the passengers or other persons I traveled with are ....

Fanny Mokotoff
(Signature of applicant)
2829 W. 33rd Street
(Address at which applicant receives mail)

Subscribed and sworn to by the above-named applicant before me at Brooklyn, New York this 8 day of July, 1930

[SEAL]

Jacob ... (Signature of attestor)
Notary Public, Kings Co. No. 138, Reg. No. 2181
Cert. filed N. Y. Co. No. 586, Reg. No. 2-M-434

Document in the possession of the author's father and discovered after his death. It is an application for a Certificate of Derivative Citizenship for his father's mother, Fanny Mokotoff. Filled out by her, it includes information she personally provided including her place and date of birth, ship and date of arrival in the U.S., mother's maiden name, name of person to whom she was coming (her brother), and street address at the time the application was made (July 8, 1930).

that time." Conclusion: 1937 (my birth year) less 35 years demonstrates my grandparent's were married about 1902.

I once interviewed my mother's cousin and had a similar experience. I asked the man when his grandparents were married. He said he did not know. Sometime later I asked him if he had photos of his grandparents. "Yes," he said, "in fact, I have a photo album from my grandparents' 50th wedding anniversary in 1941." 1941–50=1891.

Going through my father's personal effects with my mother after he died, I discovered a photograph of a woman with two young children. My mother claimed it was my father's aunt: "You know, the one who lived in California." My mother was wrong. Fortunately there was a message written on the back of the photo in Yiddish. It said:

> *My dear sister Frieda [my grandmother Fanny]*
>
> *I am sending you my picture. I am asking you to send me your picture. I thank you all. From me Sara Centner.*
>
> *For remembrance sake, Surele with Yankele and Tzipa Centner. 1914 6/7.*

Sarah Centner and children

This was an important photo. I remembered as a child that my father told me his mother had a sister who was murdered in the Holocaust. This was a picture of her, and now I had evidence of her married name: Sarah Centner. Many years later it led to my finding the descendants of Sarah Centner who survived the Holocaust because they went to Eretz Yisrael (today's Israel) in the 1920s. The mother (with her husband) and little boy remained in Poland and did not survive.

Sample Interviews That Actually Occurred

Case Study: Determining Dates Relative to Life Events

"Do you know when your grandfather died?"
"No."
"Was he alive when you were born?"
"Yes."
"Was he alive when you were bar mitzvahed?"
"Yes, in fact he died a year later."

Case Study: Given Names of Ancestors from Living Persons

"Do you know the name of your grandmother?"

"No, she died before I was born."

"Whom are you named after?"

"My grandmother."

Ashkenazic Jews—the Jews from Central and Eastern Europe—name their children after deceased relatives. Asking relatives whom they are named after may provide clues to ancestors. I did not start my genealogy career to discover the names of my ancestors but to prove that every Mokotoff in the world is related to me. (They are.) In 1979, I received an unsolicited letter from Israel from a man who was not related to me. It said that I had an unusual name—Mokotoff—and included in the letter were the names and addresses of every Mokotoff in the Israeli telephone book. I sent 11 letters to Israel asking, "Are we related?" As people responded, I asked them for the names of their ancestors. All had a father or grandfather named Tuvia—except my family. Some months later, as I was speaking to my father's cousin, I stated that I knew the Hebrew names of all my great-uncles except one, Joe Mokotoff. I asked the cousin if he knew what Joe's Hebrew name was. He pondered for a while and then said, "Oh yes, I remember. It was Tuvia." This clue eventually led to the discovery that all Mokotoffs in the world are descended from my great-great-great-grandfather, Tuvia David Mokotów, and his two wives: Tauba Moskowicz and Sarah Israelowna.[3]

Summary

Living relatives and family friends have knowledge about your family history. Interview them and ask the questions that will jog their memory. Be sure they do not just give names but dates and places of births, marriages and deaths. Be sure to get maiden names of married women.

When interviewing people use a recorder. Take notes and match these notes against the recorded interview. You will be surprised how much information was given that is not included in your notes. Listening to the recording may remind you of questions you forgot to ask, and a second interview may glean additional information.

[3] The women's surnames are actually patronymics (based on the name of their father).

Records of Your Ancestors

Genealogical research is accomplished primarily by finding documents of your ancestors. It is virtually impossible for someone to have existed on the face of this Earth without leaving some trace of his/her existence. Our ancestors were born; there may be a birth record. Our ancestors were married (at least mine were); there may be a marriage record. Some of our ancestors are no longer alive; there may be a death record. An ancestor may have owned real property, been in the military, voted in an election, paid taxes, participated in a census, been mugged (police records and newspaper accounts) or was a mugger. All these events create documentation of your ancestors. It is your role as the family historian to locate these documents and add newly found relatives to the family tree—citing the source of the information.

Vital Records

Today, virtually every country records the vital events of its citizens: births, marriages and deaths. These events are usually recorded in the town hall where the event occurs, and is kept there for some period of time before finally being transferred to the governmental archival system. How long they remain in the possession of the town varies by jurisdiction. Most governments also have privacy restrictions and will not make these records available to the public until a specified period of time has passed since the event. Typically, birth records are considered private for the longest period of time—100 years is not uncommon. Marriage records usually have a lesser time restriction and death records the least.

Vital records include date of the event, the name(s) of the person(s) involved and the names of parents, including maiden name of mother. Death records may show place of interment and name of informant.

These records often are the starting point to push your known ancestry back one

Last Name	First Name	Middle	Birth Date	Mother Maiden	Father Last	Sex
MOKOTOFF	FANNIE				WLODAWER	F

Birth Place	Death Place	Residence	Death Date	SSN	Age
REST (OTHER)	LOS ANGELES(19)		09/10/1958		68 yrs

Indexes to vital records not only provide valuable information about the person but supply information that can be used for an application to obtain a copy of the actual record. This example is from the Rootsweb.com California Death Index.

more generation. If you know the name of a grandparent, but not the name of that grandparent's parents, finding the birth record will accurately show the names of the parents. Finding a death record will also show the names of parents but may not be correct because the informant did not have good knowledge of the information.

To determine how to acquire vital records, use Google with keywords "vital records" and the government entity. Examples: vital records Missouri; vital records Poland. Many governments, as well as genealogy-oriented organizations, are placing indexes to vital records on the Internet once they are no longer subject to privacy regulations. A few even include the actual digitized records.

Case Study: *The death record of my great-grandfather, Hyman Mokotoff, indicated his father's name was Menachem Mendel and his mother's name was Pesa. The father's name was confirmed by the tombstone inscription which stated in Hebrew "here lies Chaim Meir son of Menachem Mendel." Pesa may have been a third wife of Menachem Mendel because, many years after acquiring the death certificate, I acquired the birth record of Hyman which showed his mother's name was Rachel Leah.*

Case Study: *The death certificate of Hyman's wife, Gussie, who was also born a Mokotów, showed her father's name was George and her mother's name was Betty. Neither parent ever came to the United States. What the informant provided were the given names of a nephew and niece of Gussie who were named after her parents. "George" was actually Godl, and "Betty" was Beila Ruchel.*

Social Security Death Index. A valuable genealogical resource is the Social Security Death Index. It lists every American with a Social Security number who has died since 1962, except for those who died within the past three years. The complete index is located at <https://familysearch.org/search/collection/1202535?collection NameFilter=true> and can be searched at no charge. (See example in "Illustrations" chapter.) It provides the birth and death date of the individual (sometimes month/year only), last place of residence and Social Security number. The birth date should be accurate, because it was supplied by the decedent when s/he applied for a Social Security number. The state where the number was issued identifies that the person lived in that state at the time when s/he applied for Social Security.

The place of last residence can be a clue as to where to get the death certificate since people usually die near where they lived.[4] There is a link at the site to apply to the Social Security Administration for the original application of the deceased. It may include valuable information such as the names of parents and place of birth (often only a country). Another link brings you to a site where the actual death certificate can be ordered if it is in the public domain.

Case Study: *To fill in the birth/death dates of distant cousins who are no longer alive, I use the Social Security Death Index to capture the information.*

---

4 If a person did not die in place of last residence, the death certificate exists in the state where the person died.

Federal Census Records

Every government takes a periodical census of their population, usually every 10 years. These records are made available to the public after a number of years, usually 100. In the United States, they are available after 73 years; the 1930 census was made available in 2003; the 1940 census was released in 2012.

U.S. censuses starting with 1850 give the name of every person in the household, relationship to head of household, sex, age, marital status and occupation. For Jewish-Americans, the most valuable censuses are the 1900, 1910, 1920 and 1930 ones, since the ancestors of most Jewish-Americans came to the U.S. after 1881 (the 1890 census was destroyed in a fire). Additional information on these censuses includes year of immigration and whether naturalized (Al=Alien, Pa=Applied but not naturalized, Na=Naturalized). The 1920 and 1930 censuses also include year of naturalization which can be a clue as to where to get these documents. The 1940 census is not very valuable for Jewish immigrant research. Because the U.S. was in the Great Depression, questions asked focused on economic matters.

Censuses may take you back one or more generations. Finding your most distant ancestors in a census when they were very young reveals the names of their parents and their ages. Then finding these parents in earlier censuses when they were children reveals the names of their parents.

Each column in the census can provide valuable information about the people and even provide clues where to search next. (See example in "Illustrations" chapter.)

Address. Provided is the exact street address where the family lived at that time. Since the census taker went up and down the street/road, glance at the family names of persons living near your family to see if there are clues that other families listed are related, for example, because they have the same surname.

Name. The name on the census is the name as given by the family member providing the information. It is not uncommon for young children to be enumerated by an affectionate name. My father was born Jacob Mokotoff in 1914. In the 1920 census his name is Jake. In the 1930 census his name was the one he used in his adult life, Jack. My mother had two older sisters, Peggy and Sally. In the 1910 census they are shown by their birth names, Rebecca and Sadie.

Relationship to head of household. If lucky, a mother-in-law may be living in the household, thus giving the maiden name of the wife. A brother-in-law, however, could be the brother of the wife or the husband of the husband's sister.

Age at last birthday. Often inaccurate. In fact, comparing a number of censuses, it is not uncommon for inaccurate ages to be given. A person who was 10 in the 1910 census, might be enumerated as 22 in the 1920 census and then 28 in the 1930 census.

Month/year of birth. This appears only in the 1900 census and is likely the most accurate.

Information Provided on U.S. Censuses Applicable to Genealogy

	1880	1900	1910	1920	1930	1940
Address	x	x	x	x	x	x
Name	x	x	x	x	x	x
Relationship to Head of Household	x	x	x	x	x	x
Sex	x	x	x	x	x	x
Color or race	x	x	x	x	x	x
Age at last birthday	x	x	x	x	x	x
Month/year of birth		x				
Marital status	x	x	x	x	x	x
Age at first marriage					x	*
Number of years of present marriage		x	x			
For women, married more than once (Y/N)						
Number of children born to woman		x	x			*
Number of children currently living		x	x			
Place of birth	x	x	x	x	x	x
Place of birth – father	x	x	x	x	x	*
Place of birth – mother	x	x	x	x	x	*
Year of immigration to U.S.		x	x	x	x	
Number of years in U.S.		x				
Naturalized (Na), first papers (Pa), alien (Al)		x	x	x	x	x
If naturalized, year of naturalization				x		
Occupation	x	x	x	x	x	x
Industry			x	x	x	x
Employer, employee, self-employed			x	x		
Number of months unemployed	x	x	x		x	x
Amount of salary earned						x
Whether able to read or write	x	x	x	x	x	
Mother tongue			x	x	x	*
Able to speak English		x	x	x	x	
Whether veteran			x		x	*
Blind; Deaf and dumb	x		x			
Idiotic; insane; maimed, crippled, bedridden (separate questions)	x					
Home owned or rented		x	x	x	x	x
If owned, free or mortgaged		x	x	x		
Place of Residence April 1, 1935**						x
Value of home or monthly rental					x	x
Attended school within past year	x	x	x	x	x	x
Highest grade completed						x

* Only for a sample of the population

** For persons not in U.S., this always shows country and sometimes town.

Marital status. A status of "W" (widow) is the most likely explanation for a woman to be the head of household.

Age at first marriage (1920/1930 censuses). This, combined with year of immigration, is valuable to determine if an immigrant ancestor was married in the U.S. or in the Old Country.

Number of years in present marriage (1900/1910 censuses). Of value comparable to "age at first marriage," above.

Number of children born to woman/Number of children currently living (1900/1910 censuses). Demonstrates there were children who did not survive childhood.

Place of birth/Place of birth-father/Place of birth-mother. Valuable in identifying which ancestors were the immigrant ancestors. Can demonstrate that the couple was married in the Old Country if the eldest children were not born in the U.S. It is important to note that the country of birth represents the geography of the time the census was taken. It would be unusual to see the country of birth in the 1910 census to be Poland, since Poland did not exist as a separate country from 1795–1918. In the 1910 census, the very common Polish Christian surname Wisniewski identified 57 people who claimed they were born in Poland, 453 stated Russia and 553 stated Germany (today's western Poland).[5] The 1920 census, two years after Poland was reborn as a country, showed 1,447 Wisniewskis born in Poland, 302 in Russia and 197 in Germany.

Year of immigration (1900–1930 censuses). Very important in assisting to locate immigration records, specifically passenger arrival records (normally Ellis Island). The year of immigration is often inaccurate and should be considered approximate. It can be assumed that if the immigrant arrived within three years of a census, s/he probably gave the correct year.

Naturalization (1900–1930 censuses). One of three abbreviations. (Na) immigrant is a naturalized citizen. (Pa) immigrant has only started the naturalization process. "Pa" stands for (First) Papers. (Al) immigrant is an alien and has never applied for citizenship.

Number of years in U.S. (1900 census). Provides no more information than Year of Immigration noted above.

Year of naturalization (1920 census). Valuable to help locate naturalization papers. Often it is as inaccurate as year of immigration, especially if the year was in the distant past.

Other information on various censuses. Occupation, industry, employer, salary, whether able to read or write, mother tongue, able to speak English, whether veteran, blind, deaf and dumb, idiotic, insane, maimed, home owned or rented, owned free or mortgaged, value of home, owns a radio set (1930), lives on

---

[5] Source: Ancestry.com

a farm, attended school. The answers to all these questions breathe life into the individual and make the person more than a statistic.

Non-Federal Censuses

States have taken censuses of their population usually in a year ending in "5." Use Google to search for a particular state. The information supplied in state censuses is often similar to the federal census. The advantage of a state census is that it may be closer to some milestone date, such as immigration date.

Naturalization Records

If your ancestor was naturalized after 1907, his/her naturalization application and approval may contain a wealth of information. With the huge wave of immigrants coming to the U.S. starting just before the beginning of the 20th century, the U.S. government became more and more curious about the nature of these immigrants who came and wanted to become citizens. Prior to 1907, naturalization information provided little information beyond the name of the applicant and the country to which he was disavowing allegiance.

Becoming naturalized in the U.S. is a two-step process. First, the immigrant filled out a Declaration of Intention (sometimes called "first papers") to become a citizen and then, after clearing all the hurdles, s/he filled out a Petition for Naturalization. Once approved, the person took an oath of allegiance to the United States and was given a Certificate of Citizenship.

Information on the Declaration of Intention includes, name, address, city/town of birth, date of arrival in U.S., name of ship (obviously not for Canadian border crossings), name of wife, birth date of wife, names of children, ages (or dates of birth) and places of birth. (See example in "Illustrations" chapter.)

Beginning in 1907, the U.S. government started confirming that the immigrant arrived legally. A government worker would go to the manifest for the ship on which the immigrant claimed s/he arrived, and s/he would confirm that the immigrant was on the ship. The worker filled out a form called a Certificate of Arrival, and it became part of the naturalization papers. The document is extremely valuable, because it shows the name of the immigrant as it appeared on the manifest. This is the best source to determine the immigrant's name which was changed after arriving in the U.S.

The Declaration of Intention was accomplished by the immigrant providing a clerk the necessary information. If the immigrant had a heavy accent, the information was often recorded based on what the clerk heard. Places of birth in Eastern Europe were written phonetically. Przedzborz was written as Pshedborsh; Warka became Vurka.

Naturalization records are sometimes hard to find, because there were many courts that were allowed to perform the naturalization process. An immigrant may have been naturalized in a local federal court or a county court. More and more of the indexes to naturalizations as well as the actual documents are appearing on the Internet.

Check the names of witnesses. They may have been relatives.

Case Study: *My maternal grandparents were immigrants who were very proud they were now Americans. I recall as a child asking my grandmother for her birth date. With a twinkle in her eye, she would say, "July 4." The naturalization record of my grandfather shows it was actually July 7.*

Passenger Lists

Passenger lists have the potential of providing important information to get around brick walls in family history research. They include the name of the person as it was in the Old Country and may include place of birth; place of residence in Old Country; name, address and relationship of person from whence immigrant came; name, address and relationship of person to whom going. Other background information includes occupation at time of migration, age (often inaccurate) and marital status. (See example in "Illustrations" chapter.)

Passenger lists for all major ports and an accompanying index exist on Ancestry.com as a fee-based service. The most important passenger lists, those of Ellis Island from 1896–1924, are available free of charge at <libertyellisfoundation.org>. However, this site should not be used to search for ancestors. Instead, the Stephen P. Morse portal at <stevemorse.org> should be used, because it provides significantly more search options. (See Stephen P. Morse chapter.)

Finding your immigrant ancestor may be very difficult, because the name in the Old Country most likely was not the same as in the U.S., if nothing else, in the way it was spelled. A name as simple as the given name Abraham may have been represented on the ships manifest as Abraham, Abram, Avram or Abe. A man named Jacob may have sailed to the U.S. using his Yiddish name, Yankel. A surname such as Cohen could have been Cohen, Kagan or Kohen. Furthermore, there is the risk of misspelling or erroneous extraction of the name during the indexing process. All these considerations have been minimized when using the Morse site to search the Ellis Island database. (See "A Strategy for Using the Morse Site to Search the Ellis Island Database" in the Stephen P. Morse chapter of this book.)

Case Study: *On the manifest for the ship that brought my paternal grandfather to the U.S., he is not listed as Morris Mokotoff but as Moishe Mokotów. My maternal grandfather is listed as Judel Taratotsky, not the name he assumed in the U.S.: Abraham Friedberg.*

Case Study. *Furthermore, the passenger arrival record of Moishe Mokotów indicates that his parents lived at #6 Krochmalna Street in Warsaw, the only document that shows where my great-grandparents lived when they migrated from the Mokotów ancestral town of Warka to Warsaw. In his novel, "In My Father's Court," the noted Yiddish writer, Isaac Bashevis Singer, states that his father held court at #10 Krochmalna Street. So this author's family history includes the fact that his ancestors were neighbors of Isaac Bashevis Singer's family.*

Other Resources

Cemetery Records. Some years ago, at a family reunion of my wife's father's family, I approached the then patriarch of the family and said, "Uncle Abe, isn't it wonderful that a member of the family is documenting the Auerbach family history." Uncle Abe pondered my comment for a short while and replied, "Yes, it is wonderful, but she's a bit *mishugah* (crazy)." I asked him why he felt that way. "Because she takes pictures of tombstones," Uncle Abe replied.

Cemetery records can fill in a number of blanks on a family tree. They have the burial date of the deceased and the name of next of kin. The tombstone usually includes the exact date of death (sometimes only by the Hebrew calendar) and either the date or year of birth or age at time of death. Probably the most valuable piece of information on a Jewish tombstone that has a Hebrew inscription is the name of the deceased's father. (See example in "Illustrations" chapter.) In Hebrew, the inscription will include the following statement: "Here is buried <given name> <son/daughter of> <father's given name>." When I began my search for the Mokotoff family history, my father was able to take me back three generations, because he knew the name of his grandfather. But he did not know the name of his great-grandfather. He knew where his grandfather was buried, so a trip to the gravesite disclosed the tombstone which read: "Here lies Chaim Meir (Mokotoff) son of Menachem Mendel.

Cemetery records usually include name/address of next of kin. My experience is that Jewish cemeteries will not release this information, but they will forward a letter to that person. An alternative solution to locating next of kin is that most Jews are not buried in private plots but are buried in a portion of the cemetery purchased by a Jewish association such as a synagogue or burial society. These organizations are more likely to release the name and address of the next of kin.

Old City Directories and Telephone Books. Annually companies publish telephone books and, before telephones were commonplace, they published city directories. (For a number of years both city directories and telephone books were published.) They are of historical value because they provide the address where the individual lived at a certain time. They may also be valuable if a family cannot be found in a census, because the name is misspelled in the index. Searching the census by street address may locate the family.

Compiled Genealogies. Your family history may be done! Tens of thousands of family histories have been done; some are in print. Check the JewishGen Family Finder and Family Tree of the Jewish People (see JewishGen chapter) for other persons doing research on your family name. Family trees also exist at <ancestry.com>, <familysearch.com>, <myheritage.com> and other sites. Google your family name with the word "genealogy" for clues as to whether some distant cousin has already started the process of documenting your family and posted information on the Internet. *Sourcebook for Jewish Genealogies and Family*

Histories (Avotaynu, 1996) identifies compiled genealogies for more than 10,000 Jewish surnames and indicates where these genealogical records can be found.

Military and Draft Records. Any form filled out by a person may include their address, date/place of birth. The draft registration records of World War I are an example. They are available on the Internet at Ancestry.com. Also located at the site is World War II enlistment information as well as an unusual record group: World War II "Old Men" draft registration. This registration took place in 1942 for all men born between April 28, 1877, and February 16, 1897.

> ***Case Study:*** *The World War II "Old Men" draft registration record of my grandfather, Abraham Friedberg, indicated he was born on September 1, 1884, in Volkavitta (Volkovysk), Russia (now Belarus).*

Newspaper Obituaries. Obituaries not only provide the date of death of a person but, of greater value, names of relatives of the deceased. It is one of the best sources for the married name of the decedent's daughters and granddaughters. Many newspapers have online editions from which you can retrieve an obituary. Google the name of the decedent and the word "obituary" to try to locate a notice. Ancestry.com also has an obituary database.

> ***Case Study:*** *This obituary, placed in the New York Times, gives the names of all descendants of the deceased, including the married names of daughters and granddaughters. "Mokotoff, Milton M., Hon., Age 84, of Sands Point, New York, died on Sunday, August 19. After sixty years of marriage, he remains adored by his wife, Shirley. Beloved father of Tama Bernstein, David Mokotoff and Elaine Viders. Treasured grandfather of Marne Roskin (Thomas), Alexis and Leah Bernstein, Benjamin and Michael Mokotoff, Jared and Zachary Viders, and great-grandfather of Zoe Rose Roskin. Valued father-in-law to Michael Bernstein, Jay Viders and Susan Mokotoff."*

Probate Records. People who have assets usually have a will. The act of processing the will through the court system is known as probate. Wills disclose names of heirs who are usually close relatives. In most jurisdictions, probate records are public documents. The records are in the jurisdiction of the person's last legal residence.

Synagogue and Jewish Fraternal Society Records. Personal experience indicates these records are of little genealogical value. Membership lists typically have little information of value for family history research.

Telephone Directories (online). Want to contact a relative and don't know his/her e-mail address? Use the old-fashioned way: telephone the person. There are online telephone directories for virtually every country in the world. Search Google for "<country name> telephone directory." My preference for the U.S. is <www.whitepages.com>. It includes reverse and address lookups.

Voter Registration Records. Yet another example of the document trail left by an ancestor is voter registration records. They will not only provide date of birth, but in the case of an immigrant ancestor, the court where the immigrant was naturalized.

***Case Study**: My maternal grandfather, Abraham Friedberg, lived his entire life on the Lower East Side of New York (Manhattan). Checking the indexes of all courts that would have serviced that area yielded no record of his naturalization. A letter was sent to the Board of Elections of New York City asking for his voter registration giving his residential address. The voter registration information received showed he was naturalized in 1927 in Bronx County. There is no logical reason for him to have been naturalized there. I conjectured that since he came to the U.S. in 1905, if it took him 22 years to get naturalized, it might indicate that the bricklayer's union, of which he was a member, may have decided one day to gather up all the unnaturalized workers and got them naturalized so they could vote for the Democratic party.*

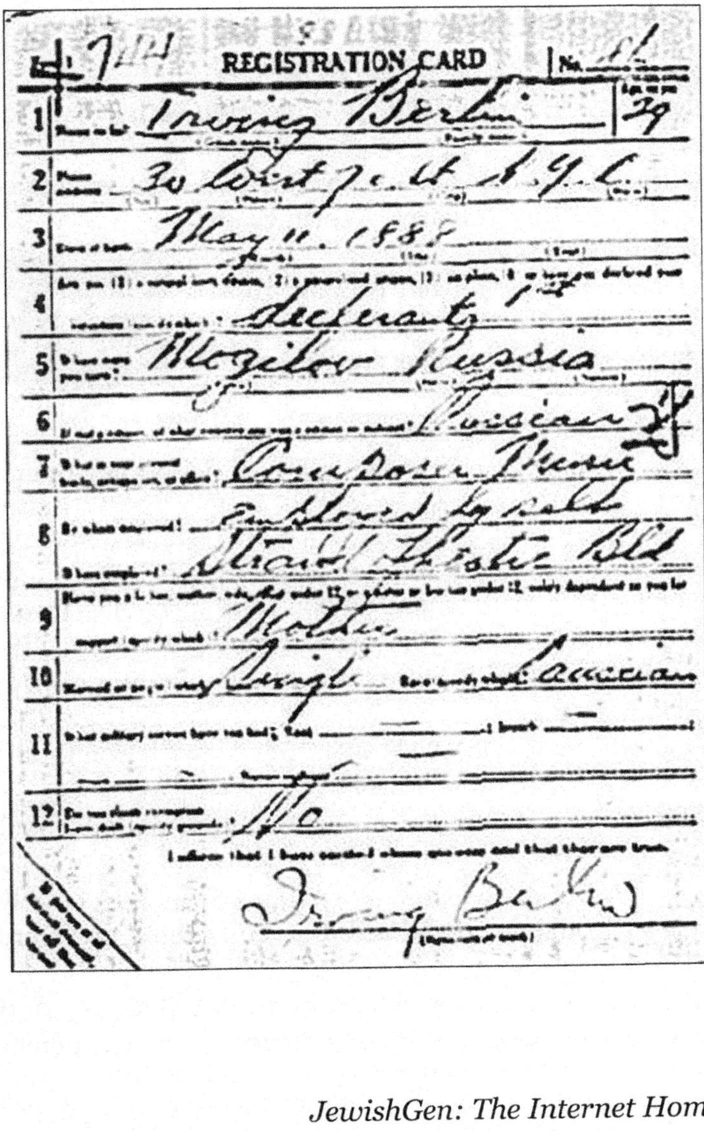
REGISTRATION CARD

1 Irving Berlin 29

2 30 West 70 St N.Y.C.

3 May 11 1888

4 Declarant

5 Mogilev Russia

6 Russian

7 Composer Music

8 Employed by self

Strand Theatre Bld

9 Mother

10 Single Caucasian

11

12 No

I affirm that I have verified above answers and that they are true.

Irving Berlin

World War I draft registration record of composer Irving Berlin. It shows that he was born in Mogilev, Russia, on May 11, 1888.

JewishGen:
The Internet Home of Jewish Genealogy

The principal presence of Jewish genealogy on the Internet is JewishGen. It receives more than 800,000 visits a year. Its presence is so vast—more than 150,000 pages—that hours can be spent just browsing the various parts of its website. At the top of the JewishGen home page at <www.jewishgen.org> are dropdown menus that link to the principal components of the site.

About Us

An outline of how JewishGen operates. Its various sections are not immediately significant to the beginning researcher.

Get Started

• First Timer. An overview of how to do family history research with a slant toward Jewish research

• Frequently Asked Questions (FAQ). JewishGen's version of what resources are available to do Jewish family history research. Worth reading once you have finished reading this book.

• InfoFiles. A directory of resources organized by both topic and country of ancestry

• Tools. Various utilities such as calendar converters and computing distance between two points

• Online Genealogy Classes. JewishGen regularly offers education programs to assist people in their research. Many are of use to beginners. Example: Basic 1 – Search Strategies

Databases

• JewishGen Family Finder (JGFF). A database of 500,000 surnames/towns being researched by more than 100,000 family historians throughout the world

• Family Tree of the Jewish People (FTJP). More than 7 million names of people that appear on submitted family trees

• Town Finder. Resource to help locate ancestral towns. See "Jewish Communities Database: below.

• Holocaust Database. Collection of databases containing information about Holocaust victims and survivors.

• JewishGen Online Worldwide Burial Registry (JOWBR). Data and possibly photos from Jewish cemeteries throughout the world. Currently there are more than 2.3 million graves identified in 104 countries.

• JewishGen Memorial Plaques Database. A database of more than 128,000 names and other information from synagogue yahrzeit plaques and other memorial records, worldwide.

• Complete List of Databases. List of databases of general interest and then primarily organized by country

Research

• Yizkor Book Project. Volunteers are translating these Holocaust memorial books into English.

• KehilaLinks. Web pages devoted to individual Jewish communities. There are currently almost 1,000 communities represented.

• ViewMate. A place to post photos and documents for identification, analysis or translation

• Special Interest Groups (SIGs). Organizations oriented primarily by country or region of ancestry provide information about their area of interest

• Hosted Groups. Jewish genealogy groups who use JewishGen's Internet servers for their websites or to store their databases

• Discussion Groups. Places to post messages and have them viewed by thousands of subscribers

Donate

JewishGen is a volunteer organization that survives and grows based on financial contributions to the organization

Volunteers

JewishGen is primarily a volunteer organization with thousands of individuals providing the data and services. There is an expression among Genners that if you find something missing from JewishGen, then do it yourself. JewishGen is financed entirely by voluntary contributions. Through their JewishGen-erosity program people contribute money to maintain the site and make it grow.

Logging In

To use virtually any service in the JewishGen environment requires registration as a user. Information requested is full name, postal address and e-mail address. Each user selects a password. This information is shared with no other organization, and even JewishGen rarely uses the e-mail addresses. Each person is assigned a unique control number. Future uses of JewishGen require the user to log in with his/her control number or e-mail address and password.

Searching JewishGen Databases

Most JewishGen databases give you the option to search for data that Sounds Like, Phonetically Like, Is Exactly, Starts With or Contains the provided information.

The "Sounds Like" option allows searches using the Daitch-Mokotoff Soundex

System (See Appendix A). This scheme combines spellings that sound the same and is especially valuable when searching surnames. Family names can be spelled a variety of ways. For example, the name Mokotoff is used in English- and Spanish-speaking countries. In Israel it is spelled Mokotov, and the original Polish spelling, Mokotów, is still used by some Holocaust survivors. Using the Sounds Like search will cause all these spelling variants to be found in the same search. There is a potential disadvantage to soundex searches; the results may contain many false positives, that is, results that clearly do not represent the item being searched. For example, searching for the surname "Teitelbaum" not only produced results of Teitelbaum, Tejtelbaum, Titlebaum, Teutelbaum, Taytlebaum but also Dattelbaum. Clearly Dattelbaum is unlikely to be a variation of the name Teitelbaum, but because in soundexing the letters "T" and "D" are synonymous, they are part of the same result. JewishGen has implemented a feature that helps to eliminate these false positives. If you place a letter or letters in brackets ([ ]) it means the exact letter must be present, not its soundex equivalents. So a search for [T]eitelbaum would eliminate any name that starts with the letter "D." Use this feature only if it is absolutely certain that the correct letter is known. (*Z*uckerman can also be spelled *Ts*ukerman and *C*ukierman.)

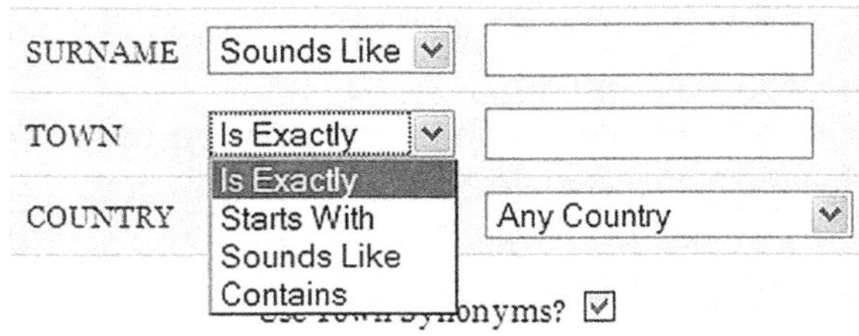

The search box from the JewishGen Family Finder shows the typical four options for searching databases: Is Exactly, Starts With, Sounds Like and Contains.

Beider-Morse Phonetic Matching (BMPM) is an algorithm that also searches for results that are phonetically equivalent to the desired name but uses a different approach than the Daitch-Mokotoff Soundex System (D-M). In BMPM, from the spelling of the name, an attempt is made to determine the language. Phonetic rules for that particular language are then applied to transliterate the name into a phonetic alphabet. If it is not possible to determine the language with a fair degree of certainty, generic phonetic rules are used instead. Finally, language-independent rules regarding such things as voiced and unvoiced consonants and vowels are applied to further insure the reliability of the matches.

The disadvantage of the D-M system is that it tends to generate false positives—results that are clearly not similar to the requested search. The disadvantage of the BMPM is that it tends to generate false negatives—omit meaningful results. Which should be used? Try the D-M approach first. If the results are so extensive and unusable, try the BMPM system.

The "Is Exactly" option means just that; the database must have the exact spelling. This is especially valuable for town names where the spelling is certainly known. For example, it would be unwise to search for a town that Sounds Like "Paris" or "London," since the spelling is known.

"Starts With" can occasionally be useful. Searching for surnames that Start With "Mokoto" not only would produce results for Mokotoff, Mokotów, and Mokotov, but also Mokotowski.

The "Contains" option is of limited use. It requires that the search argument contain at least five characters. Search for "owski" would locate any surname that ends in "owski" (or appears any other place in the name).

JewishGen Family Finder (JGFF) http://www.jewishgen.org/jgff/

One of the most valuable resources for Jewish genealogy is the JewishGen Family Finder. It is a database of ancestral surnames and towns being researched by more than 100,000 genealogists throughout the world. The database can provide the user with a list of persons researching the same surname and/or the same ancestral town. Persons researching the same ancestral town may have knowledge of resources for locating documents of the people of the town. Similarly, a person researching the same surname may know where there are records peculiar to a given surname. A person researching the same surname in the same town may be some previously unknown distant relative who has already done much of your family history.

On the previous page is the search dialogue for the JewishGen Family Finder. To determine which persons are researching a particular surname, type the name into the box on the surname line. Use the "Sounds Like" option, because there may be spelling variants of a surname. As noted above, the names Mokotoff, Mokotov and Mokotów are used in different countries for the same surname. Leave the box "Use Town Synonyms?" checked unless you know the exact spelling of the town as it exists today. Without that option, a city such as "Warsaw" will produce no results because the correct spelling is "Warszawa."

Name	Born	Died	Father + Mother	Code
MOKOTOW, Kayla Sora	1840		Jakob + Ruchla Lenemanow	1001
MOKOTOW, Kielman	1903	1943	Joshua + Hana Hildebrand	1001
MOKOTOW, Lachlan Isaac	Living		Steven John + Samantha Weinstein	1001
MOKOTOW, Lachlan Isaac	Living		Steven John + Samatha Weinstein	2784
MOKOTOW, Laia	1833		Moshe + Chaia Sarah Nusbaum	1001
MOKOTOW, Laia	1856		Hirsik + Sura Webner Wajberg	1001
MAGDOFF, Laura				5692

Results of a JGFF search show the surname as spelled by the submitter, town name and country, and, in most cases, the name of the submitter. The results may also provide the postal address and always an e-mail link to the submitter. E-mail addresses are not shown, because they could be harvested by a third party. (See example of JGFF results in "Illustrations" chapter.)

Family Tree of the Jewish People (FTJP)
http://www.jewishgen.org/gedcom/

This is a database of more than seveen million people located on family trees provided by submitters. Results include the name of the person, birth and death year, names of parents and JewishGen control number of submitter. For privacy purposes, if the person is living, birth year is omitted and replaced with the word "Living."

Clicking on the person's name provides a three-generation chart which shows the individual's parents, spouse(s) and children. Information provided for each individual on the three-generation chart includes exact dates and places of birth, death and marriage. If the person is living, birth information is omitted. There is also a link on the page which allows you to send an e-mail to the submitter.

Special Interest Groups (SIGs)

Special Interest Groups (SIGs) are an essential part of the JewishGen environment. These groups are organized primarily by ancestral region. Three are non-geographic: Rabbinic, Sephardic and Yiddish Theatre/Vaudeville. The geographic SIGs are Austria-Czech, Belarus, Bessarabia, Bialystok Region, Courland, Danzig/Gdańsk, Early American, French, German, Hungary, Latvia, Łódź area, Romania, Scandinavia, Southern Africa, Sub-Carpathia, Ukraine, United Kingdom and Warszawa. Four SIGs are independent organizations but are hosted by JewishGen. They are Gesher Galicia, Jewish Records Indexing–Poland, Litvak (Lithuania) SIG and Suwalki-Lomza SIG. Each has its own web environment within JewishGen that provides data specific to its region or interest.

Most have their own force of volunteers growing databases and other content specific to their needs.

Discussion Groups
http://www.jewishgen.org/JewishGen/DiscussionGroup.htm

JewishGen began in 1985 as a Message Board. Now this function is merely a component of JewishGen. In the Discussion Groups, researchers can share information, ideas, methods, tips, techniques, case studies and resources. Most important they can be used to post queries about individual research that hopefully

Portion of the results page of the Family Tree of the Jewish People searching for "Mokotoff" using the soundex option. Information provided includes name, birth and death year, father's and mother's names, and the code number of the person submitting the information.

can be answered by another subscriber. (See example in "Illustrations" section.) Each Discussion Group has an archives of all messages previously posted. The main group—JewishGen Discussion Group—has every message posted since 1993. Search the archives for ancestral towns and names to see if there have been previous inquiries.

InfoFiles
http://www.jewishgen.org/InfoFiles/

Volunteers have written articles about various aspects of Jewish genealogical research either by topic or country.

Currently there are articles about the following topics: Basics, Books & Periodicals, Cemeteries, Genealogical Techniques, Genealogists, Genetics, Holocaust, Immigration, Internet Sources, JewishGen Resources, Libraries & Archives, Military, Miscellaneous, LDS (Mormon) Resources, Names, Postal Matters, Preservation, Rabbinic, Seminars, Sephardim, Social Security, Special Interest Groups, Translation, Transliteration, Travel and Vital Records.

Geographic areas included in articles are: Argentina, Australia, Austria, Belarus, Belgium, Brazil, Canada, Croatia, Czech Republic, Denmark, Finland, France, Germany, Hungary, Ireland, Israel, Italy, Latin America, Latvia, Lithuania, Moldova, Netherlands, Norway, Poland, Romania, Russian Empire, Slovakia, South Africa, Sweden, Switzerland, Ukraine, United Kingdom and United States.

Nearly all of these topics have more than one InfoFile. For example, under the topic of Names, the following articles appear: Jewish Given Names–Slide Presentation, Names of the Jews (Preliminary FAQ), Bibliography on Jewish Given Names, Jewish Given Names Databases, Alternate Surnames in Russian Poland, Soundex coding–National Archives and Daitch-Mokotoff .

JewishGen Online Worldwide Burial Registry (JOWBR)
http://www.jewishgen.org/databases/cemetery/

JewishGen would like to create a database of every Jewish burial site in the world, ideally with a photograph of each tombstone. To date, volunteers have provided information about more than 2.8 million burials. They are searchable at the JOWBR site.

JewishGen Memorial Plaques Database
http://www.jewishgen.org/databases/memorial/

A database of more than 128,000 names and other information from synagogue yahrzeit plaques and other memorial records, worldwide.

JewishGen Communities Database
http://www.jewishgen.org/Communities/

This site has three major components:

JewishGen Online Worldwide Burial Registry - Australia

Burial Record

Run on Tuesday 18 February 2014 at 10:03:30

Name (Other Surnames)	Place of Birth / Place of Death	Date of Birth / Date of Death	Hebrew Name / Hebrew Date	Age / Burial Date
MOKOTOW, Hersh	Warsaw	18-Feb-1919	Zvi Herschel Ben Yehuda	89 yrs.
		30-May-2008	25 Iyyar 5768	01-Jun-2008

No Image Available

Plot	Spouse	Father / Mother	Comments	Cemetery Name / City / Country
Section 10, Row J, Plot 24, 1		Yehuda Ben Hersch		Melbourne Chevra Kadisha - Springvale /
		Rachel Bat Moshe Leib		Melbourne / Australia

Jewish Online Worldwide Burial Register includes an entry for a Mokotow family member who was a Holocaust survivor. He immigrated to Australia after World War II. Note that this unusual record provides three generations of names. His father's name was Yehuda and his grandfather's (father's father) name was Hersch.

- Search for Jewish communities (JewishGen Communities Database)
- Search for places by name (JewishGen Gazetteer)
- Search for places by location

JewishGen Communities Database. Information about more than 6,000 Jewish communities in Europe, the Middle East and North Africa.

JewishGen Gazetteer. Any town located in Europe, the Middle East or North Africa, no matter how small, can be found through this database. It contains more than 3 million names. The source of this database is the U.S. Board on Geographic Names, which documents every populated place and geographic feature in the world providing the latitude/longitude of each location.

Search for places by location. This can be valuable if you cannot find a town but you know the name of a nearby town or major city. The feature will search for any town located within a certain distance of a given latitude/longitude within a range of 1–30 miles (or kilometers). Because the database includes every minor town, a large number of hits can be generated. There is an option to restrict the results to towns that start with a specific letter(s) of the alphabet.

KehilaLinks
http://kehilalinks.jewishgen.org/

Individuals have created websites on JewishGen that provide the history of their ancestral towns. To date, nearly 1,000 towns have been documented. Information provided can include location, Jewish population before Holocaust, history, cemeteries, links to research resources, photographs, books and articles.

ViewMate
http://www.jewishgen.org/viewmate/

This tool permits uploading images such as photos, letters, tombstone images or documents in any language and request volunteers to translate or comment on these images.

Yizkor Book Project
http://www.jewishgen.org/Yizkor/

An important resource for Holocaust research is the memorial books known as yizkor books; most are written in Hebrew and Yiddish. This project is working toward translating the works into English.

Learning Center
http://www.jewishgen.org/education/

Online courses to improve one's skill in family history research.

Tools
http://www.jewishgen.org/jos/

Currently includes:

- Calendar converter that will convert between secular and Hebrew dates
- Distance/Direction calculator between two latitudes/longitudes
- Jewish calendar creator showing holidays during the year
- Soundex code calculator for Daitch-Mokotoff and American soundex systems

Other Activities

There are other projects under the JewishGen umbrella:

- **Holocaust Global Registry**. Described as a site that provides a central place for anyone searching for Holocaust survivors, survivors searching family members or friends, and child survivors searching for clues to their identity.
- Links to sites that offer **DNA testing**.
- **Ellis Island Database**. See chapter on "Stephen P. Morse One-Step Site" for using the Ellis Island database located on JewishGen.
- **Missing Identity**. Helping child survivors of the Holocaust find their identity.
- **Forgotten Camps**. The history of German concentration camps, work camps, police and transit camps.

Stephen P. Morse One-Step Site: <www.stevemorse.org>

In April 2001, the Statue of Liberty/Ellis Island Foundation placed the Ellis Island passenger lists from 1892–1924 on the Internet with an accompanying index to the 24 million immigrants who passed through the port during that time period. The search engine to find people in the Ellis Island Database was poorly designed. It allowed searching by name, secondarily providing search capability on additional information in the database.

Two weeks later, Stephen P. Morse of San Francisco announced the development of a superior search facility that allowed searching the database in one step. It permitted users to qualify the person being searched by any number of factors including name, age at arrival, birth year, arrival year, gender, marital status and other categories. Furthermore, because Morse used a duplicate copy of the database that was in the possession of JewishGen, his site allowed for phonetic searches of surnames—extremely important for locating Jewish immigrants whose names on manifests may have had any one of numerous spelling variants—as well as searching by providing only a portion of the name.

The One-Step site was an instant success. Morse proceeded to use his talents to develop portals to other genealogically relevant websites where he felt the native search engine was inadequate. In addition, he developed utility programs that assist in genealogical research. Today, the Morse site has more than 200 functions; following highlights some of them. View the actual site for a complete list of the functions. Important note: Those items at the site that are preceded by "$" are tools that access sites that require payment of a fee. There is no charge to view the Morse site nor is there a requirement to register.

Ellis Island Search Forms and Ship Arrivals. Use the Gold form to search for immigrants. The function "Ellis Island Manifests (a/k/a Missing Manifests) (1892–1924)" allows browsing the digitized copies of the ship manifests. This is of possible value when the record for the immigrant cannot be found but the ship's name and arrival date of the immigrant is known. Use the "Ship-Lists" link to determine what ships arrived on what dates. Confirming the arrival date of a ship is important, since your source may not be accurate.

Castle Garden Years (1855–1891) Plus Other New York Arrivals. Immigrants arriving in New York prior to 1892 were processed through a different facility called Castle Garden. This section of the Morse site provides some of the functions present in the Ellis Island section for immigrants of the earlier period.

Other Ports of Immigration. Similar functions for immigrants arriving in Baltimore, Boston, Galveston, New Orleans, Philadelphia, San Francisco and Canada. Also emigrants who left through the port of Hamburg, Germany. There is also a name index to the books/databases *Germans to America, Italians to America* and *Russians to America*.

U.S. Census and Soundex (1790–1940). Not only the ability to search U.S. census by name, but also by street address through "Unified One-Step 1880 to 1940 Census ED Finder."

Canadian and British Census. Primarily provides additional search functions beyond those possible at the actual census site on Ancestry.com.

New York Census. A finding aid for New York City censuses. Enter an address and the Assembly District, Election District and the Family History Library microfilm number are provided.

Births, Deaths and Other Vital Records. Superior portals to a number of online vital records databases. Two are worth noting. "Birthday and Related Persons" accesses websites that allow locating persons living in the U.S. For a small fee, it is possible to get someone's mailing address and phone number. The New York Groom and Bride Indexes not only allow locating individuals in these indexes, but once located, can often provide the name of the spouse (bride's name in the case of the Groom Index and groom's name in the case of the Bride Index). It also provides the microfilm number for the film located at the Family History Library. Many others.

Calendar, Sunrise/Sunset, Maps. Various utilities such as converting between secular and Jewish calendar, U.S zip codes, Canadian postal codes, U.S./Canadian area codes, and international phone codes. If a tombstone only has a Hebrew date on it, the secular date can be derived from the function that converts the Hebrew date to secular date. Many others.

Dealing with Characters in Foreign Alphabets. Transliterate between English and Arabic, Greek, Hebrew, Japanese, Russian and Yiddish. There is also a *ketubah* (Jewish marriage contract) generator.

Holocaust and Eastern Europe. A potpourri of utilities.

Genetic Genealogy (DNA). Various utilities associated with DNA research.

Creating Your Own Search Applications. How to build a search engine at your website.

A Strategy for Using the Morse Site to Search the Ellis Island Database

The Morse site has functions which permit searching for immigrants who came through Ellis Island from 1892–1924. Immigrants who arrived at a different time must be searched for using Morse's "All NY Passengers (1820–1957)" function which accesses Ancestry.com, a fee-based site. The principal difficulty in locating Jewish immigrants in the Ellis Island database (EIDB) is the likelihood there were many spelling variants of the name or the immigrant changed his/her name after arriving in the United States. A name as simple as the given name Abraham

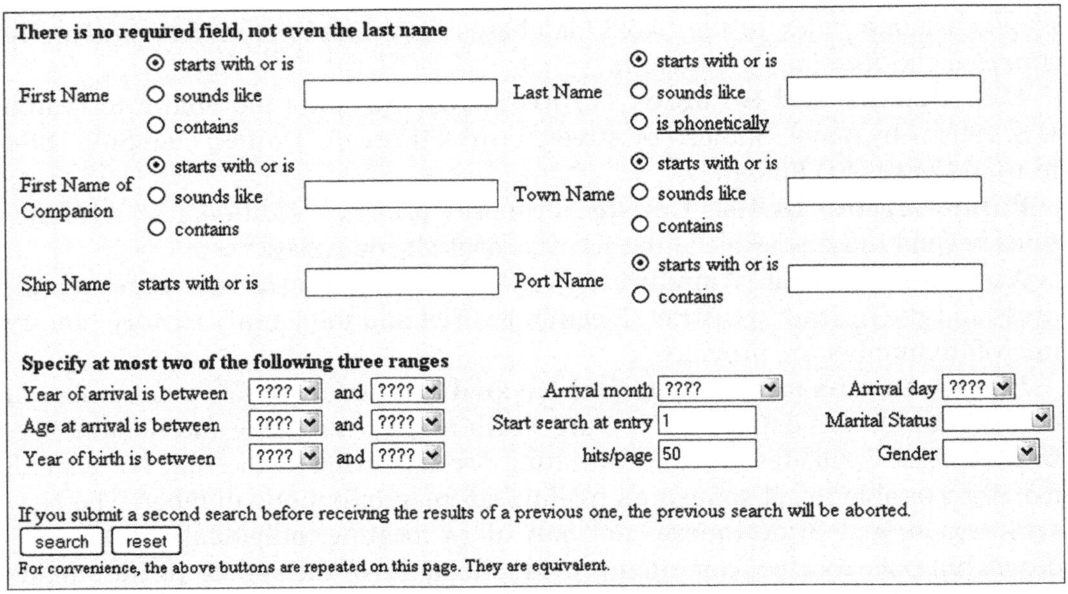

There is no required field, not even the last name

First Name ⦿ starts with or is ○ sounds like ○ contains

Last Name ⦿ starts with or is ○ sounds like ○ is phonetically

First Name of Companion ⦿ starts with or is ○ sounds like ○ contains

Town Name ⦿ starts with or is ○ sounds like ○ contains

Ship Name starts with or is

Port Name ⦿ starts with or is ○ contains

Specify at most two of the following three ranges

Year of arrival is between ???? and ????

Age at arrival is between ???? and ????

Year of birth is between ???? and ????

Arrival month ????

Start search at entry 1

hits/page 50

Arrival day ????

Marital Status

Gender

If you submit a second search before receiving the results of a previous one, the previous search will be aborted.

search reset

For convenience, the above buttons are repeated on this page. They are equivalent.

Search screen for the Ellis Island Database Gold form. Shown are all the optional parameters with which it is possible to search the database. Not shown is the lower portion of the form which is a series of check-off boxes to identify the ethnicity of the immigrant.

may have been represented on the ship's manifest as Abraham, Abram, Avram or Abe. A surname such as Cohen could have been Cohen, Kagan or Kohen. Furthermore, there is the risk of misspelling or erroneous extraction of the name during the indexing process. The Stephen P. Morse portal is so flexible that, if enough information is known about the immigrant, it is unnecessary to give his/her name at all.

Searching for an immigrant who came in the three-year span 1904–1906 who was 3–5 years old, Jewish, male and whose surname began with "S" produced only 1,045 hits, a very manageable number in this age of high-speed access.

Below is a strategy for using the EIDB based on personal experience of using the database for a great number of years.

First name. Leave it blank unless it is absolutely certain what the given name was at time of arrival. In this case, only include the initial letter(s) of the name. Eastern European Jews came using their Yiddish name; Jacob Cohen may have come as Yankel Cohen. Searching even with only the initial letter "J" will not locate him.

Last name. Try using the complete name, but elect the "sounds like" option. If the name is not found, try again using only the initial letter(s) of the name and the "starts with" option. If the "sounds like" option provides too many false results, try the "is phonetically" option.

First name of companion. Never use.

Town name. It is typically unwise to use this field, since it can be inaccurate and subject to a great number of misspellings. This author has found within the Ellis Island database more than 100 variants of "Buenos Aires, Argentina." It might be used if (1) initial results generate too many hits and (2) The place of residence in the Old Country is clearly known. In this case, only give the initial letter of the town name and use the "starts with" option.

Ship name. If this is known, it can be very valuable in finding a person when a last name search produces no result. Example. Provide a list of all Jewish men whose last name starts with "M" who came on the *Graf Waldersee* in May 1907.

Port name. This author has never found a need to use this data field.

Year of arrival. This is a valuable field to limit the number of results. If the year of arrival is "known," specify the year ± one year. If the year is believed to be known or is a guess, specify the year ± five years.

Age at arrival. It is better not to use this field, especially for persons under the age of 16. Passage costs were lower for children, and parents may have lied about age to get a lower fare. For children, place a limit of 20 years old to exclude adults. For adults, place a floor of 15 years old to exclude children.

Year of birth. A valuable field because it will exclude people who clearly are too old or too young. Use the rule shown in "Year of arrival" above regarding range of years if year of birth is known or believed to be known.

Arrival month. Do not use unless arrival month is known from reliable documentation.

Arrival day. Do not use. The exact day of a ship's arrival can be error prone.

Ethnicity. If the arrival is known to be after 1904, check "Jewish." There are cases where Jews are listed as "German" or "Russian," but this is extremely rare.

Case Study Using the Morse Site to Search the Ellis Island Database

Looking for the Ellis Island arrival record of my great-grandparents Hyman and Gussie Mokotów, I used the Morse Gold form, filled in the Last Name field with "Mokot" and clicked the option "Starts with or is." I did not give the full name, because I did not know whether they came over as Mokotoff or Mokotów. I clicked the Ethnicity section indicating that they were "Jewish." Knowing nothing else about them, I clicked the Search button. The results produced did not include them, so I went back to the Morse One-Step form. This time I gave the full name as "Mokotów" and changed the search to "Sounds like."

More Mokotóws were displayed including my great-uncle shown as Torvie Makotow (Tuvia Mokotów), my great-uncle and great-aunt Jechiel and Ernestine Mokutaw with their children Isak and Rosa. Knowing from census records that my great-grandparents came to the U.S. between 1910–1915 , I hoped that at least the first letter of their last name was correct, so I searched again using the last name to only include the first letter "M", and changed the type of search to

"Starts with or is." Since Hyman or Chaim can be spelled a variety of ways, I elected to search for my great-grandmother and set the First Name to Sounds Like "Gitel," indicated that her gender was "Female," her Marital Status as "Married," her Year of Arrival as between 1910 and 1915, and birth year as between 1850–1860 (gotten from her death certificate). Because there was a risk that she was not classified as Jewish, I removed that checked box.

Success! There were four hits:

- Gittel Maller of Glecbreio, Russia
- Helen Godell Means of Boston, Mass.
- Gittel Metger of ...uszyki, Austria
- Gittel Monkohoff of Warschau, Russia

The last entry is my great-grandmother, with two misspellings. Warschau (with an *s*) is the German spelling of Warsaw (she left from Bremen, Germany). As to the spelling of her last name, the *t* of Mokotoff got changed to an *h* for some reason. The *n* of Mo*n*kotoff apparently was the way Jews from Warsaw, including my ancestors, pronounced the name. This was told to me by a Holocaust survivor from Warsaw. (My great-uncle, Joe [Tuvia], is listed in the Ellis Island Database with last name of Mankotow.)

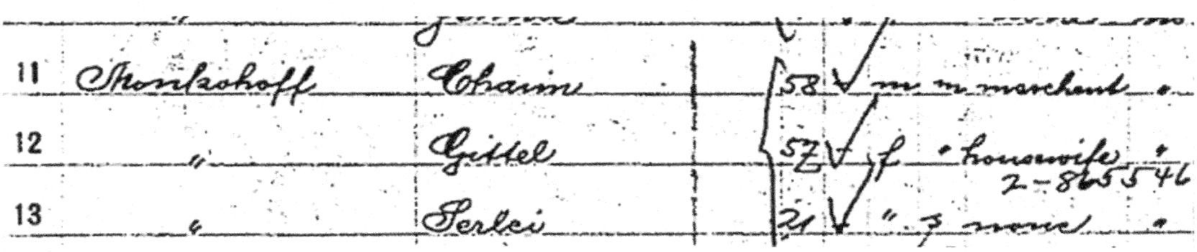
11	Monkohoff	Chaim	58	✓	m	m	merchant
12	"	Gittel	57	✓	f		housewife 2-865546
13	"	Serlei	21	✓	"	s	none

Portion of the manifest of the Kroonland which arrived at Ellis Island on January 25, 1917, showing the author's great-grandparents and great-aunt. Because the surname was misspelled as "Monkohoff," it was difficult to find the entry. Furthermore, the great-aunt's given name is misspelled in the index as "Perlei." It actually says "Serlei." Her name was probably provided as "Surele," an affectionate form of Sarah. This is why finding Jewish ancestors in the Ellis Island database is so difficult; names can be misspelled or the indexing of the names can be flawed. The Gold form has the flexibility for getting around these obstacles.

Some Other Online Genealogy Sites

FamilySearch and the Family History Library System

The largest collection in the world of genealogy-related records is held by The Church of Jesus Christ of Latter-day Saints, also known as Mormons. The stated mission of the Mormon Church is the salvation of the human race both living and dead. Toward this end, for more than 100 years, they have acquired records from institutions throughout the world under the name Genealogical Society of Utah (now called FamilySearch). Publicly they state the purpose of acquiring the records is so members of their faith can determine their ancestors (now broadened to any relative, no matter how obscurely related) and baptize them posthumously (and perform other religious rites) into the Mormon faith. While some outsiders consider such a practice strange, it is an important part of the Mormon religion, and they take the matter very seriously. So seriously that many Mormons consider it a good deed to go beyond their own family and perform Mormon rites, such as posthumous baptism, on non-relatives. The official Church policy is that this is improper, but the reality is the Church looks the other way.

FamilySearch states that its records contain 5.3 billion names from all over the world, 2.4 million rolls of microfilm, and 356,000 books. They have more than 300 camera teams copying records, now as digital images rather than on microflim. Their genealogy website is located at <www.familysearch.org>.

All of the records are available to the public at the Family History Library in Salt Lake City and can be received on loan at any of the more than 4,891 FamilySearch Centers in 129 countries. To determine the Center closest to you, on the home page <www.familysearch.org>, click "Find a Center" toward the bottom of the page, and then search by state, province or country. The results will provide the name of the Center, location, hours of operation and phone number. A typical Center has microfilm and fiche readers for use by patrons as well as equipment to print from microform or copy onto a flash drive. FamilySearch is in the process of digitizing their entire microfilm collection and placing the images at their website. They expect the project to be completed by 2020. In addition, more than 200,000 volunteers are indexing these records, and the results are being placed on their Internet site, <www.familysearch.org>.

> ***Case study:*** *Earlier in this book I reported my Mokotoff ancestry. It was at the Family History Library that I found the marriage record of my great-grandparents, the death record of my great-great-great-great grandfather as well as records of the births of the children of my great-great grandparents and great-great-great-grandparents, all from Warka, Poland.*

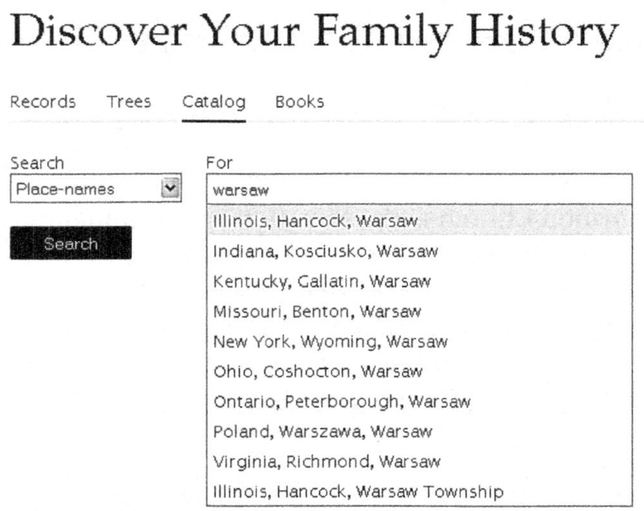

Results of searching for Warsaw provides a number of towns with the name, including the capital of Poland, which in Polish is Warszawa.

Does the Library Have Records of Your Ancestors?

Does the Library have records of your ancestors? This can be determined by using the Library's catalog. From the Home Page <www.familysearch.org>, click on the word "Search." On the following page, click "Catalog", then on the next page, type in the name of the locality being searched. If there is more than one location with the name, a dropdown menu will appear showing up to 10 locations that include the item being searched. It is not uncommon for there to be many towns with the same name. Searching for "Warsaw" results in a list of towns named Warsaw in Illinois, Indiana, Kentucky, Missouri, New York, Ohio, Ontario, Poland and Virginia (see illustration above). After confirming there are records for the town, the catalog provides a list of holdings by topic. The names of some topics include cemeteries, church records, and civil registration. There are two specifically Jewish topics: Jewish history and Jewish records. Failure to include these two topics for your ancestral town does not necessarily indicate there are no records of the town's Jews. They may appear in secular records such as civil registration, census, cemeteries and other topics.

Does the Library Have Records of Your Ancestors Online?

FamilySearch is in the process of taking all their online databases that are indexes to records about individuals and placing them in a combined database. Be sure to check off the box "Match all terms exactly." Without this feature, the results will include spelling variants that, from personal experience, will have nothing to do with the person sought.

Wildcard searches. Instead use the wildcard ability of the search engine. A

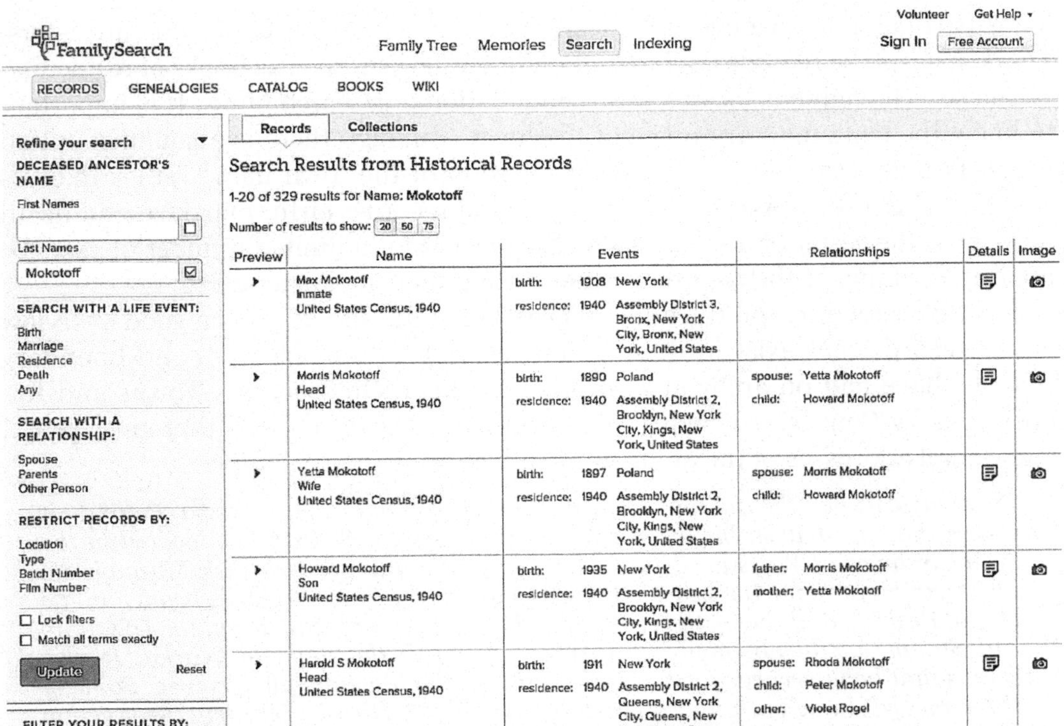

Result of searching FamilySearch for the surname Mokotoff. Note there are a total of 329 results

question mark (?) in the search field means that any single character can appear in the position of the question mark. For example, searching for M?kotoff would produce results for Mokotoff, Makotoff or any result where there is an exact match except for the second letter of the word that can be any character. An asterisk (*) is used to specify zero or more characters. For example, searching for Mokoto* would produce results for Mokotoff, Mokotow, Mokotowski, Mokotov, etc.

Routes to Roots Foundation

The most complete index to the Jewish record holdings in the archives of Belarus, Lithuania, Moldova, Poland and Ukraine is located at the Routes to Roots Foundation Internet site at <rtrfoundation.org>. The site identifies what Jewish holdings exist for each town in these countries. They may include such records as army/recruit lists, Jewish vital records (birth, death, marriage, divorce records), family lists and census records (*revizskie skazki*), voter and tax lists, immigration documents, Holocaust material, property and notary records, police files and pogrom documents, school records and occupation lists, local government and hospital records. These are Jewish records only. The absence of records for a particular town does not mean there are not records of your ancestors. There may still be records that are not uniquely Jewish, such as books of residents.

The search engine is located at <rtrfoundation.org/search.php>. It is important to know the contemporary name of the town, although there is a soundex option which permits searching by the pronunciation of the town name rather than its spelling. The most important records are vital records: birth, marriage and death records. If the result of a search lists vital records for a limited number of years or none at all, it means the records for the missing years no longer exist.

It is worth reading the Introduction section of the site. It gives a good overview of the records that exist in these countries and the impact wars and boundary changes have had on archival records of the area. One section—Towns and Repositories by Country—includes a link to the portion of the site that gives postal and e-mail addresses of the archives as well as their Internet sites.

> ***Case study:*** *For the ancestral town of the Mokotów family—Warka, Poland—it shows that the Jewish birth records for the years 1808–1872 are located in the State Archives of Warsaw Branch Archive in the town of Grodzisk Mazowiecki. The birth records for the years 1873–1899 are in the State Archives branch in the city of Radom, and the birth records for the years 1893–1939 are in the USC (Urząd Stanu Cywilnego—civil registration office) in the town of Warka. It also shows that birth records for the period 1893–1939 have not all survived. Some of these records have been microfilmed by the Family History Library. (See section on "FamilySearch and Family History Library System.")*

Jewish Records Indexing-Poland

There are numerous volunteer groups that are indexing records to assist people in their Jewish family history research. One group should be noted as exceptional. Launched in early 1995, Jewish Records Indexing–Poland is the largest fully searchable database of Jewish vital records accessible online. Located at <www.jri-poland.org> it has indexed more than 5 million Jewish birth, marriage and death records from more than 550 towns—often from as early as 1808 and up to 1915—mostly of 19th-century Poland.

The extracted information usually includes the person's name, age (for marriages and deaths), year of the event, father's and mother's name and often the maiden name of mother. Some records include exact date of the event, father's father, mother's father and ages of parents. Where the source is a microfilm located at the Family History Library, the film number is provided.

JRI-Poland is in the process of linking search results to digital images at the Polish State Archives website at <szukajwarchiwach.pl>. To date more than 1 million records have been linked. This means images of the actual documents are accessible to the user.

A personal benefit to me—being of Polish Jewish ancestry—was that my great-grandfather, the first generation to immigrant to the United States was born in Siedlce, Poland, miles away from the Mokotów ancestral town of Warka. It was discovered through the JRI-Poland site. It is unlikely I would have found the record without the index.

> ***Case Study**: I have never done research on my father's mother's family, the Wlodawers of Warsaw. Using the JRI-Poland site, I was able to trace my ancestry back to the end of the 18th century. I am Gary, son of Jack, son of Fanny, daughter of Jacob, son of Mordka, son of Jacob. Mordka's wife's name was Mindla (gotten from the index), so I tell people I am descended from Mork and Mindy Wlodawer. Given that Jacob's oldest documented child was born about 1805, according to the JRI-Poland index, it is likely Jacob was the ancestor who acquired the surname Wlodawer when the government edicted at the beginning of the 19th century that Jews would take hereditary surnames. Wlodawer means "from the town of Włodowa."*

American Joint Distribution Committee Archives

The purpose of the American Joint Distribution Committee is to assist groups of Jews in distress anywhere on the world be it from war, pogroms, epidemics, famine, revolution, or economic ruin. It was founded during World War I and was the first Jewish organization in the United States to dispense large-scale funding for international relief. It currently works in more than 70 countries.

As a consequence, the JDC Archives houses a significant collection of its efforts. It contains more than 3 miles of text documents, 100,000 photographs, a research library of more than 6,000 books, 1,100 audio recordings including oral histories, and a collection of 2,500 videos. This documentation often includes the names for individuals it has helped.

The archives has placed online at <http://archives.jdc.org/?s=archivestopnav> a database of 500,000 names found in their historic documents and client lists. Many results include the original source document that produced the result, For example, searching for "Mokotoff" identified a document dated January 31, 1919, where a Charles Mokotoff was sending $5.00 to his father Towia who lived in Warsaw.

SephardicGen.com

If researching Sephardic ancestry, in addition to the resources of JewishGen, another site will be useful: SephardicGen.com. It contains information files on how to do research, links to other sites that are Sephardic archives, discusses Sephardic research, and has family trees and news lists. There are a number of databases including one of Sephardic names, another of communities and links to offsite databases. If you have Sephardic roots, browse this site to get an understanding of what resources are available.

The developer of SephardicGen.com, Jeffrey S. Malka, is author of the definitive work on Sephardic research, *Sephardic Genealogy Second Edition: Discovering Your Sephardic Ancestors and Their World* (Avotaynu, 2009).

Encyclopedia of Jewish Genealogy

Essentially a Cyndi's List that focuses solely on links of interest to people tracing their Jewish family history. It is located at <bloodandfrogs.com/encyclopedia>. It is a new venture, created in 2016, yet it already has more than 12,000 links to online resources for more than 200 countries, and more than 80 provinces (provinces are currently only in place for Canada, Poland, the UK, and the U.S.). Each resource is in one of seven different categories: History, Genealogy, Cemeteries, Holocaust, Diaspora, Contemporary and Books.

Geni

Geni.com is a genealogy and social networking website that aims to create a family tree of the world. While most online genealogy databases are under the control of the individual that created the tree, Geni invites other members of the family to share in the experience adding facts, stories and pictures. More than 100 million profiles exist on Geni with more than 6 million users. Geni includes a mechanism to link identical people of different family trees. The hope is to show how each of us is related to the other, no matter how obscure. Geni is now a subsidiary of MyHeritage.

Cyndi's List

Cyndi's List, at <cyndislist.com>, provides links to more than 332,000 websites in 210 categories of value to family history research. It was created in 1996 by Cyndi Howells, hence its name. For example, it has 759 links in its "Jewish" category. A complete list of categories is at <cyndislist.com/categories>.

Museum of Family History

The Museum of Family History (www.museumoffamilyhistory.com) is an Internet-only museum "dedicated to preserving the history of our Jewish families, as well as Jewish history and culture, for the present and future generations." The Museum is interactive and multimedia, making available to its visitors hundreds of audio and video presentations. The subjects covered by the Museum are vast, and its numerous online exhibitions are often intriguing.

The Museum presents exhibitions about Jewish life in Europe, mostly from the nineteenth century to the present. Much can be read about Jewish immigration from Europe to such ports as Ellis Island, as well as the exhibitions about Jewish experience in the United States and elsewhere.

There are more than 100 articles from newspapers written about Jewish life in the United States more than a century ago. It has a Screening Room where you can watch video clips of more than 30 Jewish documentaries. It has an Education and Research Center, where it presents to the genealogical researcher much information about vital records and where to find them.

The Museum also has its own sub-website, the "Museum of the Yiddish Theatre," which can be found at <www.museumoffamilyhistory.com/moyt/main.htm>. The website features much material about all facets of Yiddish theatre history.

The best way to determine if there is anything of value to your family history research is to use its search engine to locate the surname and towns of interest. If, in addition, you are interested in Jewish history of the past 150 years, the site is worth a visit independent of your needs for family history research. Go to its Site Map and examine the more than 100 entries.

The Museum of Family History and the Museum of the Yiddish Theatre also have Facebook pages.

Commercial Online Genealogy Sites

Most hobbies involve spending money. Genealogy is no exception. There are a number of commercial ventures that provide valuable genealogical data to their subscribers for a fee. Access to their collection may be through a limited time-free offer, monthly/annual subscriptions and/or per record.

Ancestry.com[6]

By far the largest—and most popular site—is Ancestry.com which claims to be "the world's largest online family history resource." It has 2.4 million paid subscribers and in excess of 18 billion records from all over the world. They state their site has more than 30,000 record groups. Included are all U.S. censuses 1790–1940 and Canadian censuses from 1851–1921. Ancestry.com has all passenger lists for U.S. ports including the most important immigration port for Jews: New York 1820–1957. They have numerous naturalization indexes and some actual naturalization documents including the documents for the federal court in Manhattan, New York.

The best way to get an understanding of the scope of their collection is to go to <www.ancestry.com/search>, key in a surname and check off the box that says "Match all terms exactly." If the surname is reasonably unusual, search for a surname only. The result of the search is a list of databases that meet the search criteria and an indication of the number of records within the database. (If the display does not look like the illustration below, click the dropdown menu that says "Sorted by relevance" and change it to "Summarized by category.") In the example above, clicking on any collection name displays all the entries for the collection up to a maximum of 50 per page. If you do not have a subscription, a minimal

Immigration & Emigration	
15	New York Passenger Lists, 1820-1957
5	Index to Petitions for Naturalization filed in New York City, 1792-1989
5	U.S. Naturalization Records Indexes, 1794-1995
4	Selected U.S. Naturalization Records - Original Documents, 1790-1974 (World Archives Project)
2	Hamburg Passenger Lists, 1850-1934 *(in German)*
2	Index to Declaration of Intent for Naturalization: New York County, 1907-1924
2	New York County Supreme Court Naturalization Petition Index, 1907-24

The results of searching the rare name Mokotoff at the Ancestry.com site produces 35 records in the Immigration & Emigration section. Despite the uniqueness of the name, more than 700 records exist for the surname on Ancestry.com—not including spelling variants.

[6] Readers should be aware that the author has been retained by Ancestry.com from time to time as a consultant for Jewish genealogy.

amount of information is supplied. For example, in the New York Passenger Lists collection, only the name of the person is provided.

There are a number of other services provided at the Ancestry.com site as seen by the banner at the top of the Home Page which contains dropdown menus.

Family Trees. You can build your family tree at the site. There are currently 70 million family trees containing more than 8 billion profiles. Most people today buy genealogical software and keep track of their family history in a separate program. (See chapter on "Genealogical Software.")

DNA. Self explanatory

Collaborate. A number of functions, the most important of which is the Message Boards. It operates comparably to the JewishGen Discussion Groups described in the chapter about JewishGen.

Learning Center. Material, both written and from webinars, on how to do research

Publish. Methods of publishing the results of your research.

Shop. Books and other products Ancestry.com sells

Hire an Expert. A mechanism for retaining a professional genealogist to assist you in your research

MyHeritage

MyHeritage, at <myheritage.com> is an Israel-based company founded in 2003. Its growth has been rapid, and it is now considered a serious competitor to sites such as FamilySearch and Ancestry.com. They report having 7 billion historical records, 80 million registered users, 2.6 billion profiles and 28 million family trees. They support 40 languages.

MyHeritage

Getting started requires that you submit a family tree or start a new one. You will be asked whether you want the fee-based Premium service or the free Basic Plan. Select the Basic Plan for the opportunity to try the various features of the site. Then get the Premium service if you like what you see.

MyHeritage also offers a genealogy software system, Family Tree Builder, which can be synchronized with your online family tree. They also offer an app for iOS and Android smartphones.

What is unique about this site is the very powerful searching tools that do not exist at any other major site such as Ancestry.com or FamilySearch. When you place your family tree at their site, your tree elements are matched against all resources available to MyHeritage.

- Smart Matching™: Tree-to-Tree matches. Members of your family tree are matched against other family trees posted to the site. This is not a simple word-for-word matching but a set of sophisticated algorithms (rules) that bridge differences in spelling, phonetics and relationships that may exist between the trees. As other people add their trees, if a potential match is found, you are informed of the match. For example, a simple family tree consisting only of myself, my wife and children, giving only their names and birth dates, produced numerous matches to other trees, all relevant.

• Record Matching: Tree-to-Record matches. The 7 billion historical records in their collection are matched against all members of your tree as an example of the sophistication of their search engine, they found my name in the 1940 census even though my given name was misspelled as "Garry."

• Newspaper Matching: Tree-to-Newspaper matches. Two billion newspaper clippings in the MyHeritage collection have been extracted of all the names, dates, and facts from the articles and matched against family trees.

• Record Detective™: Record-to-Record matches. Records are flagged when they appear to relate to other family trees. If a given record appears to be a match to your tree, then the other tree is analyzed to determine the likelihood of a match.

• Instant Discoveries™: Valuable to beginners, if a match is found, other related information is noted and the user has the ability to add all the information to his/her family tree. For example, if a match is found with another tree but your tree lacks some family members, a single click will add all these members.

• Search Connect™: Every search you make is remembered. If, at some time in the future, some other person makes the identical search, both you and the searching party are made aware of the common search.

• Global Name Translation™: Names, especially Jewish names, have many spelling variants. The original spelling of this author's surname in Polish was Mokotów. In English and Spanish-speaking lands it is Mokotoff. Transliterated from Hebrew it is Mokotov. This function addresses the problem.

MyHeritage is constantly adding new technology to their site. Additional functions added in 2016 and before this book was published in September 2016 include:

• Book Matching: Tree-to-Book matches.

• Audio recordings for their mobile app which can be linked to your online family tree. Useful for interviews.

• DNA matching. Submit your DNA results to the site and it will be matched with other contributors.

• Super Search Alerts. One of the frustrating features of searching the Internet for data is that it may not be available today but is available at a later date. This feature remembers your searches and informs you if new records added to the system now match your search.

FamilyTreeDNA.com – DNA Testing

Veteran genealogists are resorting to DNA testing to prove/disprove familial relationships when other resources are not available. DNA testing is not a resource for beginners. It is a course of last resort. The primary sources should be records. Consider a neophyte genealogist named Finkelstein whose ancestors came from Radom, Poland. He locates another genealogist named Finkelstein whose ancestry is also Radom. They both submit to DNA testing and there is an exact match. What has this proven? Nothing, other than that they are closely related. It does not tell how they are related.

A possible justification for the use of DNA testing early in research is it can point you in the right direction for research. In the example above, had there been no match, time would have been wasted searching for records in the belief that the two persons were related. Equally true, if the test did prove they were related, they would have focused efforts on finding the documents that would determine the relationship.

The largest database of Jewish DNA results is at FamilyTreeDNA.com. Use this company if planning to do DNA testing. Three types of tests are offered. (1) Y-chromosome test by which males can prove/disprove familial relationship along strict paternal lines; (2) mtDNA test by which males or females can prove/disprove familial relationship along strict maternal lines; and (3) Family Finder test which can demonstrate familial relationship between two persons—independent of sex—only if they are related within five generations.

For additional information about how DNA testing works and pricing, visit <familytreedna.com>.

FindaGrave.com and Billiongraves.com

Findagrave.com contains information about more than 150 million burials throughout the world. Information may include exact dates of birth/death, cemetery location, link to an obituary and a picture of the tombstone.

Billiongraves.com limits its database to pictures of tombstones. The information in its database only has name, years of birth and death, and cemetery where grave is located. Additional information can be extracted from the picture of the tombstone, such as exact dates of birth and death. As of 2015 had 13 million records. An index to their records is also part of the FamilySearch collection.

Data for both sites are provided by volunteers. Both are worth a visit periodically to see if they have information of value to your research.

Findmypast.com

Findmypast.com has the largest collection of British records and now includes many records from Australia, New Zealand and the United States. They state there are more than 2.9 billion records in their collection. Included are:

- British census records (1841–1911)
- Index to England and Wales births, marriages and deaths (1837–2006)
- Migration records including 24 million passenger list records (1890–1960)
- Military records covering the First and Second World Wars
- Specialist records, for example, the 1925 Dental Surgeons Directory

They also have a facility to build a family tree online.

Association of Professional Genealogists

More than 2,800 people worldwide consider their profession—part-time or full time—to be family history research. They are all members of the Association of Professional Genealogists. There are a number of reasons why you might want to hire a professional genealogist:

- You cannot devote enough time to your family history research and are willing to hire a professional to do the work.
- You have hit a brick wall and want help from an experienced professional.
- Research is required in another geographic area and it would be too expensive to travel to the location.

Visit the APG site at <apgen.org>. Use the "Find a Researcher" function to locate a professional by Research Specialty (e.g. Jewish), geographic specialty (e.g. Lithuania) or location (where professional resides).

JewishData.com

Jewishdata.com is the brainchild of Avraham Laber of Albany, New York. (Albany is the capital of New York State.) It started initially with Jewish records from his local area, then expanded to include New York City and now contains a potpourri of 500,000 records and images from all over the world. Many cannot be found anywhere else on the Internet. Most notable are records and tombstone images from Jewish cemeteries across the United States, Canada, Germany and Israel. The database also includes thousands of Declaration of Intention (citizenship) documents filed by Jewish immigrants as well as rare books and other records. It is worth a visit on the chance that there are records of your ancestors. If you are a member of the Jewish Genealogical Society of New York, your membership dues includes free access to the site.

WorldVitalRecords.com

WorldVitalRecords.com, founded in 2006, is a younger version of Ancestry.com. It too offers a variety of records many of which overlap those of Ancestry.com, but others are unique to this company. They claim to have 4.2 billion names indexed. Searching for the name "Mokotoff" provided 255 hits (Ancestry.com had 488), most of which are available on Ancestry.com, except for their JewishData.com collection (see above).

Important Non-Internet Resources

Jewish Genealogical Societies and Annual Conference

There are some 75 Jewish Genealogical Societies (JGS) throughout the world. If there is one in your area, join! Typically, meetings are held once a month and there is a lecture on some topic of current interest. It also provides an opportunity to network with members and discuss research problems with the more experienced members of the society. Many societies have libraries where books on family history research are available. They also publish newsletters that can provide additional information to assist in research.

Perhaps a JGS in an area of your ancestry can assist in your research. Contact information can be found in the *Jewish Genealogical Yearbook* described below. At present, there are societies in Argentina, Australia, Belgium, Canada, Denmark, France, Germany, Great Britain, Israel, Jamaica, Netherlands, South Africa, Sweden, Switzerland, United States and Venezuela.

Most JGSs belong to an umbrella group: the International Association of Jewish Genealogical Societies (IAJGS). A complete list of societies that are members of IAJGS can be found at <iajgs.org/blog/membership/member-societies>.

Since 1981, there have been annual international conferences on Jewish genealogy, the major event of the Jewish genealogical year. Registrants from all over the world gather for six days (Sunday-Friday) to avail themselves of more than 150 lectures on various aspects of Jewish family history research. Special Interest Groups (SIG) hold meetings. There is Breakfast with the Experts, SIG luncheons and a banquet dinner. It also provides an excellent opportunity to network with other genealogy enthusiasts to discuss individual or common problems.

The schedule for future annual conferences:

2017, July 23–28, Orlando, Florida
2018, "early August," Warsaw, Poland

Avotaynu

Avotaynu[7] is a venture that focuses on the needs of persons tracing their Jewish family heritage. It is the publisher of AVOTAYNU, the quarterly journal of Jewish genealogy; *Nu? What's New?*, the Internet-based newsletter of Jewish genealogy; and more than 70 books to assist in Jewish family research. It has an Internet presence that includes a major Jewish genealogical database, the Con-

---

7 "Avotaynu" is a Hebrew word that literally means "our fathers" but has come to mean "our ancestors."

solidated Jewish Surname Index.

AVOTAYNU. AVOTAYNU is the world's largest circulation magazine devoted to Jewish genealogy. Each year, this quarterly publishes more than 250 pages of useful, interesting information that can help in your research. Its contributing editors from 16 countries throughout the world regularly gather important information that appears in its issues. The publishers, Gary Mokotoff and Sallyann Amdur Sack-Pikus, are on a first-name basis with officials at institutions containing genealogical data throughout the world, institutions such as YIVO Institute, American Jewish Archives, American Jewish Historical Society, U.S. National Archives, U.S. Library of Congress, Leo Baeck Institute, U.S. Holocaust Memorial Museum and Yad Vashem.

AVOTAYNU
The International Review of Jewish Genealogy
IN THIS ISSUE

An index to the thousands of articles that have appeared in this publication 1985–2008 can be found at <avotaynu.com/indexsum.htm>.

Subscriptions to the publication are $38 a year ($46 outside North America) with discounts for multi-year subscriptions. Ordering information can be found at <avotaynu.com/journal. htm>.

Avotaynu Anthology of Jewish Genealogy. Avotaynu has placed on the Internet all 2,900 articles published in AVOTAYNU from 1985–2011 as PDF files. A Google Custom Search indexed all the words so that if in all the articles there is only one mention of a town or a surname, the search engine will find it. By specifying key words or combinations of key words, Google locates any article that includes all of the words. Cost for accessing the back issues is a one-time charge of $35. Ordering information is at <.avotaynu.com/books/Anthology.htm>.

Nu? What's New? Avotaynu publishes the e-zine of Jewish genealogy *Nu? What's New?* weekly, usually on Sundays. A subscription, which costs $12/year can be made at <avotaynu.com/SubscribeNWN.htm>. Articles summarize recent events of interest to Jewish family historians with links to Internet sites that provide detailed information about the event. There is an archive of all past issues located at <avotaynu.com/nu.htm>. Scan the topics summarized on that page or use the search engine to locate potential items of interest.

Avotaynu Online. This is Avotaynu's presence on the Internet and is available free of charge. Register at <avotaynuonline.com>. This site is designed to publish articles that are not appropriate for the printed publication AVOTAYNU either because they are on a subject too specific to be of interest to a general audience, or too lengthy for the 68-page magazine. Being on the Internet also means there is greater freedom to include audio/video recordings and numerous illustrations. As a bonus to readers, all articles from 2007–2011 published in AVOTAYNU, the International Review of Jewish Genealogy, are available at no charge at the Avotaynu Online website.

Book Publishing. Since 1991, Avotaynu has published more than 70 books designed to enhance the user's ability to do Jewish genealogical research. Five of them have won awards given by the Association of Jewish Libraries and the Jewish Book Council. In 2004, the Association of Jewish Libraries gave Avotaynu its "Body of Work" award as acknowledgement that, collectively, its books are major contributors to Jewish knowledge. A complete list of books currently in print can be found at <avotaynu.com/allbooks.htm>. Many of the sites for individual books include the book's Table of Contents. A few also include sample pages. Some of the more notable books are:

Avotaynu Guide to Jewish Genealogy. This definitive guide to Jewish genealogical research is written by more than 60 authors, all experts in their own field. The list of authors is a veritable "Who's Who in Jewish Genealogy." Its more than 100 chapters cover all important aspects of the rich body of information available to do Jewish genealogical research.

Sephardic Genealogy: Discovering Your Sephardic Ancestors and Their World—Second Edition. The definitive guide on how to do Sephardic genealogy. This profusely documented work describes how to trace Sephardic ancestry through archives as ancient as 12th-century Spanish notarial records or as recent as today's country repositories.

Where Once We Walked: A Guide to the Jewish Communities Destroyed in the Holocaust–Revised Edition. Can't find your ancestral town? This book identifies more than 23,500 towns in Central and Eastern Europe where Jews lived before the Holocaust. Included are 17,500 alternate names such as Yiddish names and names under previous political entities. Also given is the latitude/longitude of the town, its Jewish population before the Holocaust and citations to as many as 50 books that reference the town.

A Dictionary of Jewish Surnames from the Russian Empire, A Dictionary of Jewish Surnames from the Kingdom of Poland (now out of print), A Dictionary of Jewish Surnames from Galicia, A Dictionary of German-Jewish Surnames. Are you aware that the concept of Jews having hereditary surnames—family names passed down from father to sons—is not much more than 200 years old? These four books have received world acclaim as definitive works on the presence, etymology and geographical location of tens of thousands of Jewish surnames in the named regions. The first three-named books have an extensive introductory portion that describes the origin and evolution of Jewish surnames in the particular area.

A Dictionary of Ashkenazic Given Names. Comparable to the surname books, except it is for Ashkenazic given names. The 300-page introductory portion was the author's doctoral thesis at the Sorbonne in Paris. More than 15,000 given names are included in the dictionary.

Consolidated Jewish Surname Index (CJSI). One of the frustrations in doing research is the need to check many sources for potential information about your family history, only a few of which contain information of value to your research. CJSI goes a long way to reducing the time needed to check these sources. It contains nearly 700,000 surnames that appear in 42 (mostly Jewish) databases. These databases combined contain more than 7.3 million records. The very sources discussed in this book, such as the JewishGen Family Finder, Family Tree of the Jewish People, *A Dictionary of Jewish Surnames from the Russian Empire* and Jewish Record Indexing-Poland project, are included. CJSI is sequenced phonetically rather than alphabetically using the Daitch-Mokotoff Soundex System (see Appendix A); therefore, spelling variants of a name that sound the same are grouped together. (See an example of CJSI results in "Illustrations" chapter.)

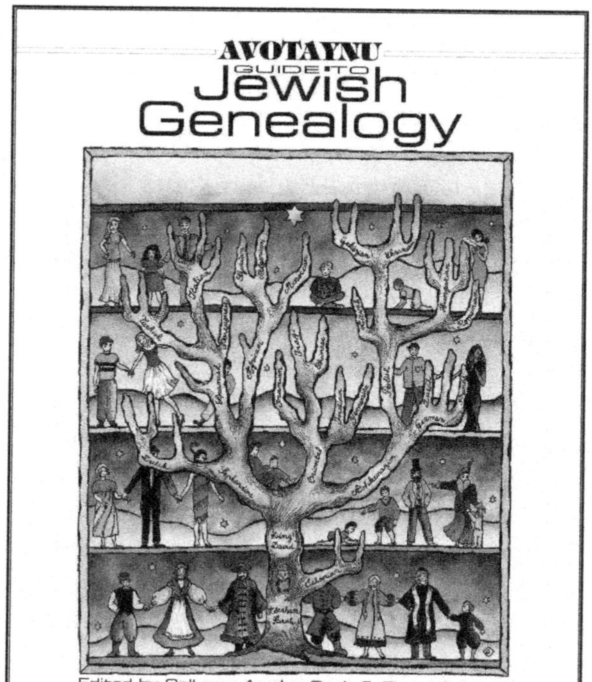

Avotaynu Guide to Jewish Genealogy is one of many books published by Avotaynu to assist people in the Jewish familyhistory research. The front cover was the source of the cover for this book.

Holocaust Research

The Nazis took away their names and gave them numbers. We genealogists are taking away their numbers and giving them back their names.
—Arthur Kurzweil

Every Jewish person with roots in Central or Eastern Europe has family members who were murdered in the Holocaust. When I first heard about the Holocaust in the 1950s, it was something that happened to Jews—other Jews. My family was safe in the United States. Then, in 1979, I began to research the Mokotów family history. To date I have documented more than 1,700 descendants of the progenitor of the Mokotów family, Tuvia David Mokotów, and his two wives, Tauba and Sarah. Of these 1,700 individuals, more than 400 were murdered in the Holocaust. I know of less than 30 survivors. If you were a Mokotów living in Poland in 1939, it was unlikely you were alive in 1945. Many Jewish genealogists consider their family history work a memorial to members of their family that perished in the Holocaust.

One of the great myths of Jewish genealogy is that all the records were destroyed in the Holocaust. While most things Jewish in Eastern Europe were destroyed, family history research relies primarily on government records, which in most cases were not destroyed. It is a tribute to the archivists of the world that, while members of the human race are constantly trying to destroy each other, archivists are constantly concerned about preserving the history of their country. As the Holocaust slips into history, many of the vital records of victims are being made public, because these people were born more than 100 years ago.

Case Study. *I am distantly related to the noted Jewish scholar, Eliyahu Kitov (born Abraham Eliyahu Mokotów). When I met his son in 1982, he informed me that his father had numerous sisters and brothers who remained in Poland and were murdered in the Holocaust. He did not know their names. Today, I have all their names and birth dates, because they were born more than 100 years ago, and the Polish State archives made the records public.*

In addition to government records, there are many Holocaust-related records that survived World War II. The Holocaust is called the most documented event in history. Literally tens of thousands of books have been written about the event; only a few document individuals. Yet they represent millions of records that are, for the most part, available to family historians.

There are three principal sources of information about Holocaust victims and survivors.

- Shoah Victims' Names Database
- International Tracing Service
- Yizkor books

	Place of Residence (or Place of Birth)					
Name	Town	District	Region	Country	Birth Date	Source
Cukerman Blima	WARSZA	WARSZAWA	WARSZAWA	POLAND	1914	Page of Testimony
Hirschfeld Sara	GARWOLIN	GARWOLIN	LUBLIN	POLAND		Page of Testimony
Maysner Faygele	WARSZA	WARSZAWA	WARSZAWA	POLAND		Page of Testimony
Mokatow Berek	FRANKFURT AM MAIN	WIESBADEN	HESSE-NASSAU	GERMANY	1892	List of victims from Germany
Mokotoff Gitta	FRANKFURT AM MAIN	WIESBADEN	HESSE-NASSAU	GERMANY	1899	List of victims from Germany
Mokotoff Israel	FRANKFURT AM MAIN	WIESBADEN	HESSE-NASSAU	GERMANY	1862	List of victims from Germany
Mokotoff Israel					1862	List of Theresienstadt camp inmates
Mokotow Morris	FRANKFURT			GERMANY	1868	Page of Testimony
Mokotow Kielman	WARSAW	WARSZAWA	WARSZAWA	POLAND	1903	Page of Testimony
Mokotow Sara	WARSAW	WARSZAWA	WARSZAWA	POLAND	1910	Page of Testimony
Mokotow Cesia	WARSAW	WARSZAWA	WARSZAWA	POLAND	1909	Page of Testimony
Mokotow Reginka	WARSAW	WARSZAWA	WARSZAWA	POLAND	1923	Page of Testimony
Mokotow Moshe	WARSAW	WARSZAWA	WARSZAWA	POLAND		Page of Testimony
Mokotow Miriam	WARSAW	WARSZAWA	WARSZAWA	POLAND	1882	Page of Testimony
Mokotow Rozka	WARSAW	WARSZAWA	WARSZAWA	POLAND	1925	Page of Testimony

Results Page: 1 2 3 4 5 Next

Partial list of people with the surname or maiden name Mokotoff (and variants) in the Shoah Victims' Names Database.

Shoah Victims' Names Database

Starting in 1955, Yad Vashem, the Holocaust memorial and archives located in Jerusalem, sent a worldwide call for people to come forward and document each of the six million Jews murdered in the Holocaust on individual pieces of paper called Pages of Testimony. The document is in two parts. The first part identifies the individual with his/her name (including maiden name of married women); year/place of birth; name of father, mother and spouse; place during war; and date/place of death. On some forms there was a place to name children and their ages, although properly each child was to appear on a separate form. The second part of the document includes the name and address of the submitter and relationship to the victim. The document is signed and dated.

To date, Yad Vashem has acquired more than three million Pages of Testimony, and the database is still growing. It could be said that half of the victims have been identified by name and circumstances.

Because the document identifies the individual making the submission, it is possible to contact that person and gather more information about the family. Unfortunately, many of the submissions were made shortly after the project started in 1955, and the submitter is no longer alive. Locating descendants of the submitter usually can provide information.

Case Study: *My maternal grandmother had a sister, Sarah Centner, who was murdered in the Holocaust. I located a Page of Testimony for her submitted by her daughter living in Israel. Using Israeli resources, I determined she was deceased, but I was able to contact her children who described all the circumstances of their family immigrating to Eretz Yisrael in the 1920s. All immigrated except* *for the parents—my great-aunt and uncle—who remained in Poland and became Holocaust victims.*

The Pages of Testimony have been digitized and indexed and are available at the Yad Vashem site, <yadvashem.org>. Click on the link to the Shoah Victims' Names Database. Other lists have been added to this database, but for the most part the names have merely been extracted. Few of the actual lists have been digitized and made available on the Internet. An example is *Gedenkbuch*, which is a list of more than 150,000 German Jews murdered in the Holocaust. It is shown in the database as "List of victims from Germany." Another example is "List of Theresienstadt camp inmates."

International Tracing Service (ITS)

Toward the end of World War II, the Allied Powers started collecting documentation of people persecuted by the German Nazi government. This led, in 1955, to the establishment of the International Tracing Service located in Bad Arolsen, Germany. This is an archives of documents about people. If ITS received a list of 723 people deported from France to Auschwitz, they created 723 index cards, one for each person. If they received a list of 7,216 people who died in the Lodz ghetto, they made 7,216 index cards, one for each individual on the list. If they had a register of 25,214 persons in a refugee camp in 1946, they created 25,214 index cards. By 1955, ITS had accumulated more than 50 million index cards that placed a specific person in a specific place at a specific time.

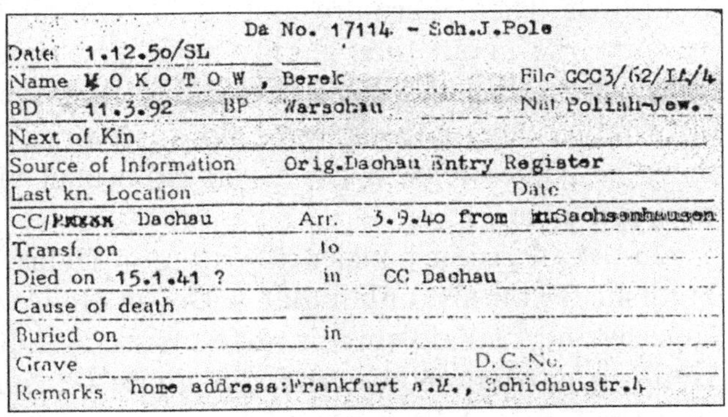
Da No. 17114 - Sch.J.Pole
Date 1.12.50/SL
Name MOKOTOW, Berek File GCC3/62/II/4
BD 11.3.92 BP Warschau Nat Polish-Jew.
Next of Kin
Source of Information Orig.Dachau Entry Register
Last kn. Location Date
CC/PKXXX Dachau Arr. 3.9.40 from xxSachsenhausen
Transf. on to
Died on 15.1.41 ? in CC Dachau
Cause of death
Buried on in
Grave D.C. No.
Remarks home address:Frankfurt a.M., Schichaustr.4

One of the 55 million index cards in the Central Name Index at ITS. It provides information about a Holocaust victim from a Dachau Entry Register.

For more than 60 years, these records were not available to the public and could only be accessed through a written inquiry to ITS. Response time from ITS was measured not in days or months but in years. In November 2007, the ITS collection was made accessible to the public and each of the 11 countries that made up the ITS steering committee were permitted to have one and only one copy of the digitized records, the Central Name Index and the software that performed searches and retrieved the records. These countries are Belgium, France, Germany, Greece, Israel, Italy, Luxembourg, The Netherlands, Poland, United Kingdom and the United States. In the United States, they are at the U.S. Holocaust Memorial Museum in Washington, DC. In Israel, records are at Yad Vashem in Jerusalem.

See their respective sites to determine how to make an inquiry.

Yizkor Books

After World War II, many survivors of the Holocaust published books that memorialized the destroyed Jewish communities of Europe. Called yizkor books (*yizkor* means "memorial" or "remembrance" in Hebrew), they commemorate the victims as well as the Jewish communities. Actually, yizkor books had been published for many years before World War II, but the term has now come to mean specifically Holocaust memorial books. To date, more than 1,000 towns have been commemorated in this manner. Yizkor books were created independently, but they have a typical format. First, there is a history of the Jewish presence in the town from its beginning to post-Holocaust. Then there are individual remembrances by survivors about their family members, especially those who perished. This is followed by remembrance of families where there were no survivors. Finally there is a necrology, a list of all Holocaust victims from the town.

Front cover of the Bialystok, Poland, yizkor book, one of the few that has an extensive English-language section.

Almost all yizkor books are written in Hebrew and Yiddish. If you are unfamiliar with the Hebrew alphabet or do not understand Hebrew and/or Yiddish, it is not a brick wall but merely a surmountable obstacle. Write, or have someone write, the family's surname in Hebrew and Yiddish. Then scan the Table of Contents of the book under the article title and author for the surname. Where there are pictures of people, scan the captions for the presence of the name. Finally, locate the name in the alphabetical necrology in the back of the book. Make copies of pages on which the name appears and have someone translate them. If you don't know anyone who reads the two languages, go to a local synagogue for assistance.

The New York Public Library has placed hundreds of yizkor books online at <http://yizkor.nypl.org>.

Other Resources

There are many resources that are specific to a particular town, region or country. Use Google to search for additional resources. For example, if your family came from Lublin, Poland, search Google using the keywords "Holocaust Lublin" to gather additional information.

Special Problem: My Name Was Changed at Ellis Island

One of the great myths of immigration to the United States is that immigrants, especially Jewish immigrants, had their names changed at Ellis Island. According to Marian Smith, former Historian for the Citizen and Immigration Service, there is no evidence that this ever occurred.

The scene of immigrants standing in line at Ellis Island shouting out their names to a non-Yiddish speaking clerk is a myth. Jews, as well as other immigrants, came with documentation indicating who they were. Their names were recorded on the ship's manifest for the very purpose of permitting U.S. immigration officials to check off the aliens as they passed through Ellis Island. The immigrant's name was written on these manifests by the ship's staff. In fact, one of the best sources for an accurate spelling of a European surname as well as the town of ancestry is the ship's manifest.

What did happen in the majority of cases is that Jewish immigrants, shortly after landing in the United States, discarded their European surnames and Americanized them for a variety of reasons.

- The most common reason was that the name—as spelled—was pronounced differently in English, so they kept the name but spelled it according to the rules of English pronunciation. Lipszyc became Lipshitz, Tartacki became Tartasky, Fajnsztajn became Feinstein, Mokotów became Mokotoff.
- Common Eastern European surname endings were dropped to "Americanize" the name. Moszkowicz became Moskow, Tartacki became Tarre, Fajnsztajn became Fine.
- Due to anti-immigrant and anti-Semitic attitudes of the Americans, they wanted to disguise their Jewishness: Chajkowski became Shaw.[8]

What can you do if your family's name was changed and no one in the family remembers the real name?

Name Changes in the United States

If the name was changed in the U.S., there are two major sources of the original name: naturalization and passenger arrival records.

Certificate of Arrival. Starting in 1907, part of the naturalization process to become a citizen was that a government official checked the passenger list of the ship on which the immigrant claimed s/he arrived and verified s/he came legally to the U.S. The official filled out a Certificate of Arrival confirming the legal entry.

---

[8] The woman who told me about her name change explained to me that "in the 1920s, you could not get a job if your name was Chajkowski."

On the ship's list itself, the official wrote, next to the name of the immigrant, the date the search was made and the Certificate of Arrival number. This Certificate then became part of the documentation for naturalization. If the immigrant arrived with a different name, the name as it appeared on the ship's list often was shown on the Certificate. Find the naturalization records of your ancestor. They should show the name in the Old Country. (See Appendix B for an example of the use of the Certificate of Arrival.)

Passenger Arrival Record. A passenger arrival record approach is more circuitous. If the naturalization record does not have the original name, it will show the name of the ship on which the immigrant arrived and the date of arrival. If the ship came to Ellis Island, confirm that it arrived on the date specified at <stevemorse.org/ellis/boatx.html?mode=ny>. If it is within a day or two of the date the immigrant claimed, assume it is correct, otherwise you may have to search many arrivals of the ship in that year. Continue using the Morse site to go to the ship's manifest. Somewhere on the many pages is the entry for your ancestor with his European name. There is a column on the manifest called "Race or Nationality." In searching the pages of the manifest, only focus on persons identified as "Hebrew," which is the way Jews were identified. You likely know the approximate age and the Yiddish given name of your ancestor. Let us assume his first name was Izzie in the U.S., but his tombstone shows his name was Yitzhak. His naturalization papers (or family legend) state he arrived when he was 19 years old. You now can scan the ship's manifest for a Hebrew person, about 19 years old, whose first name was any of the European spellings of Yitzhak, including Isaac, Icek, Izik, etc. Once a possible hit is found, read the rest of the entry. Does the place of origin agree with family lore? Does the name of the person and place where he was going agree with family lore? From these facts, you should be able to locate your ancestor's entry and, consequently, his European surname.

Name Changes in Europe

If family legend states that the name was changed in Europe, you have a much more difficult task. Here is a possible strategy. First, determine the ancestral town. Then access the vital records of the town (or hire a professional researcher who has access). You must know some information about the family in Europe, such as the given names of family members. Also determine the time frame of the family's residence in the town.

Case Study: *Your great-grandfather, Morris Forlehrer, came to the United States, but family legend says Forlehrer was not his name in Europe; he changed it to avoid the onerous draft laws of the Russian Empire. It would appear that is all you know, but there is more information that can be gathered. Using the suggestions in the chapter on "Finding Your Ancestral Town," you determine he was born in Radom, Poland. Go to his gravesite and read the tombstone inscription. It says he was "Moshe ben Yitzhak; died 1935, at age 62."*

Armed with this information, you can now look at the birth records of Radom for a male child born about 1873; birth name, in Polish, likely Mosiek; father's name, likely Icek. If there are one or more records that fit this profile, the birth record will provide the mother's name. Look in other years for other children born to the couple. Jews name their children after deceased relatives. Knowing now the given names of this family unit, do they coincide with the religious names of members of your family?

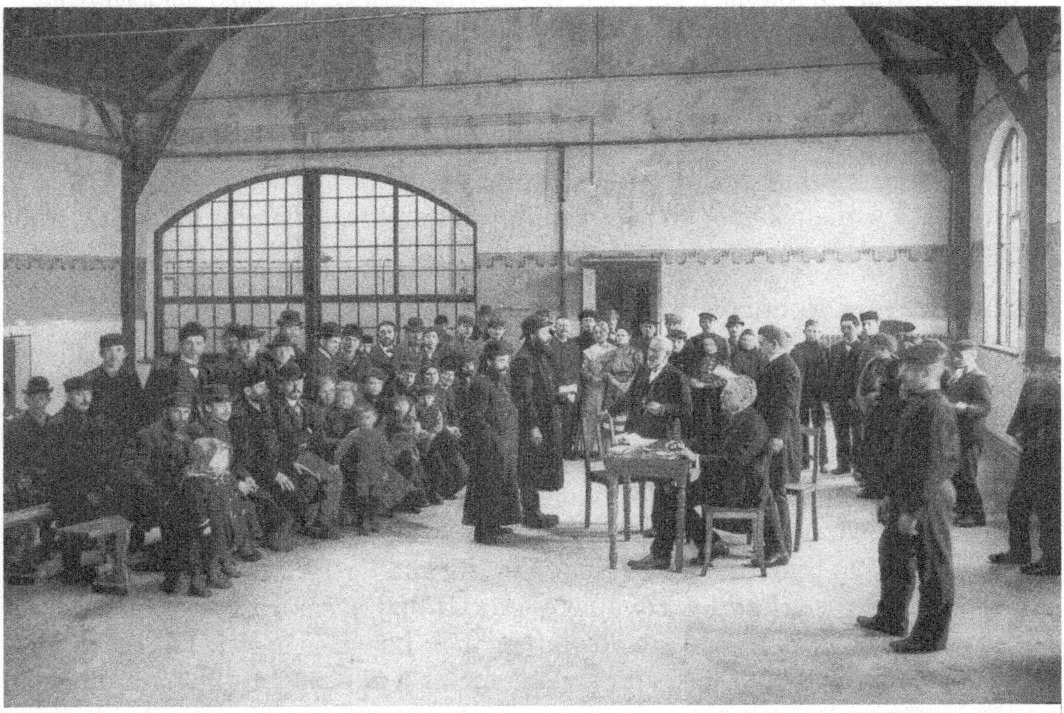

Members of the German Central Committee for Jews greet Eastern European emigrants at the port of Hamburg. Courtesy Hamburg State Archives.

Special Problem: Finding Your Ancestral Town

Many beginning genealogists do not know their ancestral town. Family lore sometimes, at best, indicates they came from Russia, Austria (meaning the Austro-Hungarian Empire) or Lithuania. There is also a risk that family legend says they came from Vilna or Minsk, but evidence eventually uncovers that this meant Vilna *guberniya* (province) or Minsk *guberniya*. This is similar to Americans who claim they are from New York. Do they mean New York City or New York State?

To further confuse the situation, if family legend says you came from a particular country, it means the country as it existed when they came to the United States. Today's Poland, at the turn of the 20th century, was not an independent country, but consisted of portions of the Russian, German, and Austro-Hungarian Empires. The area called Poland after World War I today is partially in Poland, Lithuania, Belarus, and Ukraine.

> ***Case Study.*** *A woman once contacted me stating her family came from Lemberg, Austria. Consulting a good indexed map of Austria, she could not locate the town. I informed her she was looking for Lemberg, Austro-Hungary, which today is L'viv, Ukraine.*

If you do not know your ancestral town, it is a brick wall that must be circumvented, because you will not be able to go back in time to locate records of your ancestors without this vital piece of information.

There are some primary sources of information that will help to identify your ancestral town.

Naturalization Records

Prior to becoming a citizen, your ancestor filled out an application called a Declaration of Intention (known as First Papers). The information also appears on the Petition for Naturalization (known as Final Papers). One question asked of applicants was, "Where were you born?" That is the good news. The bad news is that the clerk preparing the document invariably wrote what he heard as the name of the town. With a thick Yiddish accent, town names can be distorted. The good news is that there is a gazetteer of Central and Eastern Europe, *Where Once We Walked: Revised Edition* (Avotaynu, 2002) that has a soundex index (an index arranged by how a word sounds rather than how it is spelled) of the 35,000 town names in the book. Take the town name as it appears on the naturalization papers, soundex the name, and look it up in the soundex index of the book. From the choices in the soundex index, determine your town. Alternately, JewishGen has a Jewish Communities Database at www.jewishgen.org/Communities/Search.asp that performs a comparable function.

If your family memorabilia includes the Certificate of Citizenship of your ancestor, the document will state the court in which your ancestor was naturalized. Contact the court to determine where the naturalization documents are now kept. Many have been microfilmed by the LDS (Mormon) Family History Library (see chapter on this facility) or are available on Ancestry.com or Fold3.com.

Passenger Arrival Records

Since the early 19th century, when a ship came to the United States, it was required to provide a list of passengers to the authorities. These lists are available online at Ancestry.com or FamilySearch.com. If your family came through Ellis Island after 1895, it is best to search for their record using the Stephen P. Morse One-Step site (see chapter on this subject). Passenger arrival lists, after 1893, contain a column for Last Residence, which might be town, province, or country, depending upon the ship. Lists after 1906 added birthplace and both city and country. If your ancestor came before 1893, passenger arrival lists will be of little use to you since they only show country of origin. Note, however, that emigration lists, notably those of the port of Hamburg, Germany, (described below) do show town of origin.

There is an advantage to using passenger arrival records as a research source compared to naturalization records; the arrival records likely have the town name spelled correctly. That is the good news. The bad news is that the name of the town is the name as it existed at the time of arrival. Due to the political changes in Eastern Europe during the past 100 years, town names changed, country names changed, and boundaries changed. Again, two valuable sources are available: *Where Once We Walked* and JewishGen Jewish Communities Database. Both have thousand of alternate names for towns. Searching by these alternate names will provide the current name and country.

Hamburg Emigration Lists

Many ports in Europe created emigration lists of people leaving their ports. Few lists have survived, and fewer are easily accessible to the public. One port where the lists survived and are accessible is Hamburg, Germany. If your ancestors came before 1896 or you cannot find naturalization records, try the Hamburg Emigration Lists which go from 1850–1934. Many Central and Eastern European Jews came through the port of Hamburg on their journey to the United States. The lists contain the name of the town of origin. They are available on Ancestry.com.

Other Sources

In addition to the major sources described above, there are a host of other documents that might contain the name of the ancestral town.

• Census records. Rarely do census records have more than country of birth, but some people have reported that the census taker sometimes accidentally included town or region. For the 1920 census, the instructions to the census takers stated they were to list the province of birth for those born in the former Russian and Austrian Empire. The instructions were not always followed.

• Vital records (birth, marriage, and death certificates). These often list place of birth, but invariably, for an immigrant, only country is shown. Again, included might be town or region.

• Burial societies. Jewish immigrants formed *landsmanshaft* societies that were social and help groups organized around a town of origin. The groups had burial committees that bought land in Jewish cemeteries and then sold plots to their members. If your ancestor was buried in a landsmanshaft society plot, it may indicate that was his/her town of birth (or that of the spouse).

• Social Security applications. When a person applied for the Social Security program, which started in 1937, a question on the application was place of birth; therefore, town of birth may be shown.

• World War I Draft Registration Cards, 1917–1918. For men born between 1886 and 1897 (whether citizens or aliens), this documentation gives the exact place of birth: city/town, state/province, country.

• Obituary notices. Items published in local secular and Jewish newspapers often contain more accurate details than official death certificates.

• Probate records. Wills and administrations can contain clues. Filed on the county level.

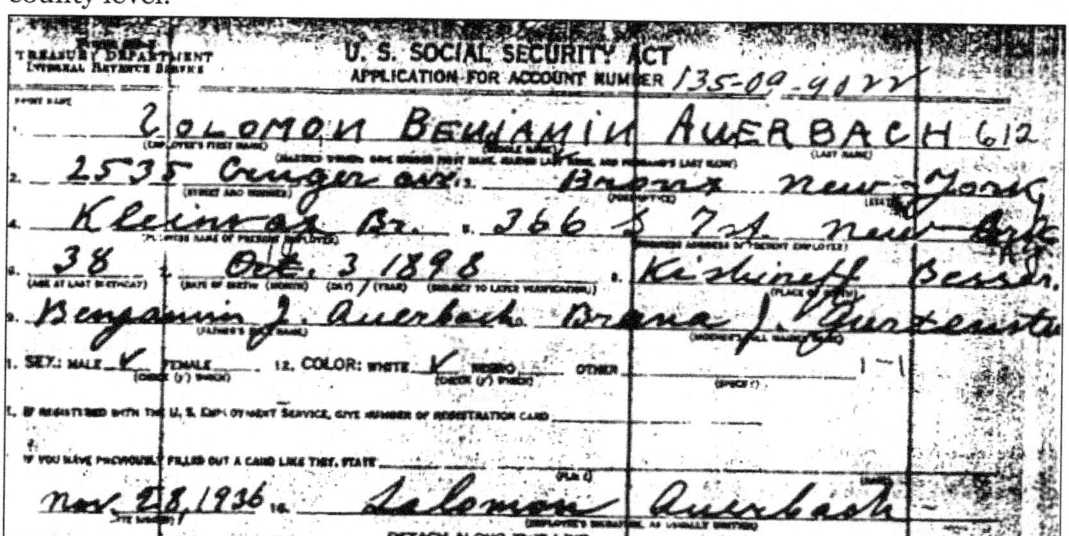
TREASURY DEPARTMENT
INTERNAL REVENUE SERVICE
U. S. SOCIAL SECURITY ACT
APPLICATION FOR ACCOUNT NUMBER 135-09-9122
Solomon Benjamin Auerbach 612
2535 Cruger Ave. Bronx New York
Kleinvar Br. 366 7 Av. New York
38 Oct. 3 1898 Kishineff Bessar.
Benjamin J. Auerbach Brana J. Gurtenstein
SEX: MALE ✓ FEMALE 12. COLOR: WHITE ✓ NEGRO OTHER
IF REGISTERED WITH THE U. S. EMPLOYMENT SERVICE, GIVE NUMBER OF REGISTRATION CARD
IF YOU HAVE PREVIOUSLY FILLED OUT A CARD LIKE THIS, STATE
Nov. 28, 1936 Salomon Auerbach
DETACH ALONG THIS LINE

Social Security Application: This application to participate in the Social Security program filled out in 1936 by an immigrant shows his parents' names (including mother's maiden name) and applicant's date and place of birth (Kishineff, Russia; today, Chişinau, Moldova).

Getting Started Properly

A common complaint among veteran family historians is "if I only had started properly." If only I had:

- Placed all my research in a database using genealogy software
- Kept track of the sources of my information
- Kept my information in a standard way
- Maintained a research log

Genealogy Software

Once the commitment is made to research your family history, it is important to document the results of the research in an orderly way. Today, with the common use of computers, it is customary to use one of many genealogical software programs available.

Genealogical software systems have a number of advantages:

- A single location contains everything known about members of your family.
- Locating an individual and the associated information is rapid using the internal search engine.
- Photographs or scanned documents can be attached to an individual's record.
- There are numerous reports that can be produced such as lists of descendants or ancestors and research-oriented reports.
- It is possible to share your data with others through a system known as GEDCOM.

Choosing Genealogical Software

The most popular genealogical software system is Family Tree Maker. It can be purchased online at <familytreemaker.com> or in stores. The current version is "Family Tree Maker 2014." If older versions are available at a lower price, it is okay to buy the older, cheaper version. Recent improvements provide additional levels of sophistication well beyond the needs of people starting to trace their family history. If there is more than one version of Family Tree Maker available, with more expensive versions offering discounts or additional software or databases, buy the cheapest version.

Interestingly, I do not use Family Tree Maker but another product called Brother's Keeper. I have been using it for more than 20 years and have no motivation to switch to a superior product. My needs are merely to store the information I know about each family member, cite the sources, attach pictures and documents to individuals in the database and produce a variety of reports. Brother's Keeper satisfies these needs.

There are scores of software systems available. Other popular packages are:

• Reunion. <www.leisterpro.com> Until recently the only decent system for the Mac. (Family Tree Maker is now available for the Mac.) Users consider it an excellent system.

• Family Tree Builder. <www.myheritage.com/family-tree-builder> Its principal advantage is that it is available in 34 languages, and data can be input using many alphabets, including Hebrew and Cyrillic (Russian).

• Brother's Keeper. <www.bkwin.net> One of the oldest of the genealogical software systems. It provides all the basic needs of recording family history information.

```
Menachem (Menkho) Tartasky
├─Unknown (Tarre cousins) Taritotzki
│  ├─Leibel Taratotski
│  ├─Chaim (Hymie) Taratotski
│  │  ├─Joseph Tarre
│  │  │  └┬Shirley Kaplan
│  │  └─Louis Tarre b.25 Apr 1904
│  │     └┬Esther ? b.May 1902 m.Apr 1933
│  └─Harry Tartasky (Gershon Taritotzki) b.1869
│     └┬Esther ? b.1867
│      ├─Louis Tartasky b.ABT 1890
│      ├─Julius Tartasky b.ABT 1891
│      ├─Bella Taratatski b.ABT 1893
│      ├─Gertrude Taratatski b.ABT 1896
│      └─Benjamin Taratatski b.ABT 1899
├─Unknown (Tarre) Tartotski
│  └─Meyer Tartatsky b.1858 d.ABT 1917
│     └┬Freide Nasovich d.1943
│      ├─Abraham Tartatsky
│      │  └┬Lena Novick b.16 Sep 1891 d.Jan 1979
│      ├─Yosby Tartatsky d.1943
│      │  └─? ?
│      ├─Mordke Tartasky d.ABT 1927
│      │  └┬Malke (Molly) ?
│      ├─Israel Tartatsky b.ABT 1882
│      │  └┬Mollie ? b.ABT 1882
│      ├─Samuel (Shlam) Tarre b.1889 d.1950
│      │  └┬Bertha Kaplan b.15 Aug 1889 d.May 1985
│      ├─Albert Tartatsky b.4 Oct 1901 d.Jan 1977
│      │  └┬Helen Seid b.16 Mar 1900 m.5 Nov 1927 d.Mar 1977
│      └─Leizer (Louis) Tartatzky b.AFT 1901
├─Yechazkel Tartasky b.ABT 1830 d.ABT 1910
│ └┬Taube ? d.BEF 1910
│  ├─Chaim Binyes Tartasky
│  │  └┬Wife1 ?
│  │   ├─Nataniel Cohen d.ABT 1939
│  │   ├─Jack Cohen
│  │   ├─Abe Cohen
```

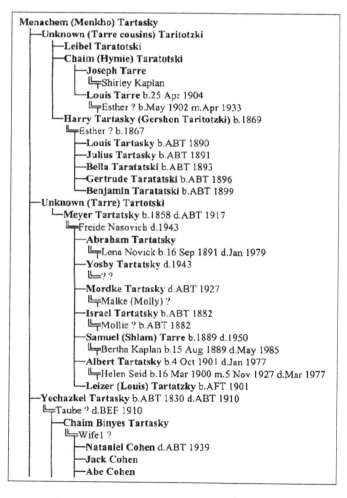

Descendancy Chart. One of the many reports and charts that can be produced by genealogical software systems. It shows the progenitor on the top line and all descendants below indenting one unit for every generation. This chart was produced using Brother's Keeper software.

Cite Your Sources

The biggest mistake neophyte genealogists make is that, as they are adding new information to the family history database, they fail to document the sources where they obtained the information. It is guaranteed that as new information is found about your family some will conflict with previously acquired data. If you fail to cite the source of the original information, you may forget where it came from which may cause wasted time relocating the source. It is important to find where you acquired this conflicting information in order to evaluate what is likely to be the accurate data.

All genealogy software programs have provisions for citing sources. As data is entered, include the source of the information in a manner that will allow you to retrieve the document if it is needed in the future. Better yet, scan the document and attach it to the person(s) identified in it.

Standards

Always write information in a standard way. Here are some recommendations:

• Names should be written as <given name> <middle name> <last name>. The name of a married woman is her birth name. (Her married name can be determined by looking at her husband's record.) For living persons, use their current name. For deceased persons, use their name at time of death. Any other names by which the person was known during his/her lifetime are placed in special fields provided by the software or can be placed in the notes section. Example: My father is shown as Jack Mokotoff. In the notes section of his record it states "Born Jacob Mokotoff."

• The format for date is <two-digit day><space><3-character month abbreviation><space><year>. Example: 03 Sep 1842.

• The place name is the name of the place when the event occurred. According to genealogical standards, U.S. places are shown as name, county, state. Example: Brooklyn, Kings, New York. Other countries should be town, province, country. Example: Warszawa, Warszawa, Poland.

A good source for the names of counties and provinces is the Family History Library catalog. Go to <www.familysearch.org/eng/Library/FHLC/frameset_fhlc.asp>. Click search by Place. Type in a town name. The results will be a list of all towns in the Library's collection (which is very complete) showing the town name, county/province and state/country.

Maintain a Research Log

Maintain a log of all resources checked including the date, description of resource and its location. If it is on the Internet, identify the URL. Include a brief description of what was found, including what was not found. A research log will eliminate duplicate effort in the future when it is uncertain whether a specific resource was checked.

Glossary

Below are some terms and abbreviations commonly used in Jewish genealogy.

ancestor. Someone from whom you are descended.

APG. Association of Professional Genealogists.

Ashkenazic. Pertaining to Jews whose origins are medieval Central and Eastern Europe.

chevra kadisha (חברה קדישא). Literally "holy society." Burial society. An organization dealing with the proper treatment of the deceased from death to burial.

Church of Jesus Christ of Latter-day Saints. Proper name of the Mormon Church.

civil registration. Registration of records by the secular government. In genealogy, it usually applies to vital records.

collateral lines. Relatives who are not your ancestors, e.g. aunts, cousins.

FamilySearch®. The Internet site of the Mormon Church that focuses on genealogy. It is located at <familysearch.org>.

Family History Center (FHC). A branch library of the Family History Library. There are approximately 4,600 FHCs in 134 countries..

Family History Library (FHL). A facility of the Church of Jesus Christ of Latter-day Saints (Mormons) located in Salt Lake City, Utah. It is the largest genealogical library in the world.

guberniya (губерния). Major administrative subdivision of the Czarist Russian Empire, equivalent to province.

HIAS. Hebrew Immigrant Aid Society. A social service organization that has helped Jewish immigrants relocate in the United States since the late 19th century.

IAJGS. International Association of Jewish Genealogical Societies. A confederation of some 73 Jewish genealogical societies throughout the world.

ITS. International Tracing Service. A facility located in Bad Arolsen, Germany, that contains millions of records of people persecuted by the Nazi regime. It is a major Holocaust archive.

JewishGen. The largest presence of Jewish genealogical information on the Internet. Located at www.jewishgen.org.

JGFF. JewishGen Family Finder. An Internet database of ancestral surnames and towns being researched by tens of thousands of Jewish genealogists throughout the world.

JGS. Jewish Genealogical Society. An organization of people located in a given geographic area researching their Jewish ancestry. There are more than 70 JGSs throughout the word.

kahal. See "kehila" below.

kehila (קהילה). Hebrew word for "community." The organized Jewish community that sets rules for its members. Also *kahal.*

ketubah (כתובה). Jewish marriage contract.

Kreis. German word for "province."

landsmanshaft society. (plural, landsmanshaftn) A Jewish social organization made up of people from the same community in the Old Country.

LDS. Latter-day Saints. Pertaining to the Church of Jesus Christ of Latter-day Saints (Mormon) Church or a member of the Church.

oblast (область). Major administrative subdivision of the USSR and today's Russia, equivalent to province.

NARA. National Archives and Records Administration. The U.S. national archives.

powiat. Administrative subdivision of Poland equivalent to "county."

raion (район). Administrative subdivision of the USSR and today's Russia equivalent to district.

relative. Someone who is connected to you by blood or by marriage.

revizskie skazki (ревизские сказки). Russian word for "revision list." Essentially a census.

Sephardic. Pertaining to Jews whose origins are medieval Spain.

shtetl (שטעטל). Yiddish word for "village." Tends to be used in genealogy to mean town of ancestry independent of size.

SIG. Special Interest Group. A Jewish genealogical organization that focuses on an area of common interest, most frequently a geographic area of common ancestry.

shul (שול). Yiddish word for "synagogue."

uezd (уезд). Russian term for district.

USHMM. United States Holocaust Memorial Museum located in Washington, DC.

vital record. A record of a life event: birth, marriage, death. Divorce records are usually considered vital records.

voivodship. (Polish, *województwa).* An administrative subdivision of Poland equivalent to "province."

Appendix A: How to Search Online Databases

With Internet access to genealogy-relevant records becoming commonplace, searching online databases properly is a skill that may yield many rewards. Sometimes a search for a specific individual produces no results even though a person actually appears in the database. A variety of circumstances may lead to this unfortunate result. The name may be erroneously indexed because the original data is misspelled; the indexer copied the information incorrectly to create the index; the researcher has used the wrong spelling of the name; the name appears in the record with a variant spelling.

Because of these potential problems, the thorough researcher must develop effective strategies to search databases. Several tactics are discussed here.

First, search for the exact name. If such a search produces no results, or the search possibly has generated incomplete results, then determine options that the site's search engine may offer for further, more refined searches. (Incomplete results can occur, for example, when searching a census for all known relatives and only some are found.)

Search Engine Options

Many search engines, especially larger ones and those whose authors recognize the possibility of spelling variants in indexes, include additional options for searching the database. These options include wildcard searches, phonetic or soundex searches, starts with/contains/ends with searches; synonym indexes; and fuzzy searches.

Wildcard Searches. Wildcard searches permit a researcher to specify that a given character or set of characters may be any letter of the alphabet. An international standard exists for wildcard searching. According to this standard, placement of a question mark (?) in a given position in a word means that any single character may occur in that position. Placement of an asterisk (*) in a given position indicates that any number of characters may appear in that position, including no characters. For example, searching the 1930 U.S. census on Ancestry.com for M?k?t?ff produces the following results in addition to Mokotoff: Makatoff, Makotoff, Mikitoff and Mukotoff. With the exception of Mikitoff, all the names referred are relatives of the author and are erroneous spellings of Mokotoff. Searching for Moko* uncovered another relative, my father, erroneously enumerated in the Ancestry version of the 1930 census as Jacob Mokodoff.

Phonetic/Soundex Searches. Names sometimes are written according to that which a writer hears rather than the correct spelling. Names also may have changed during the immigration process to accommodate pronunciation patterns in the new country. The Polish Jewish surname Minc (pronounced *mintz*) typically is spelled Mink or Mintz in the United States. The Polish surname Mokotów (pronounced *mukutoof*) is spelled Mokotoff in English and Spanish-speaking countries. Systems developed to account for these spelling changes are known as soundex or phonetic searches. In 1985, this author and Randy Daitch created the Daitch-Mokotoff Soundex system, which is commonly used in Jewish genealogical databases. For a description, see www.avotaynu.com/soundex.htm.

Starts with/Contains/Ends With. The "starts with," "contains" and "ends with" search options may be useful if a portion of the name to be searched has an unusual string of letters and, therefore, is not likely to produce a large number of results. The function of these search options is identical to the wildcard asterisk (*) option. Using Mokotoff as an example, the searches are represented by Mokot*, *okot*, and *toff, respectively.

Synonym Indexes. This rare search engine function usually applies to given names and produces results for synonyms of a given name. The Shoah Victims' Names database at yadvashem.org has this capability, for example. Searching for a woman named Rebecca produces results for women identified as Rikula, Risa, Riva, Rivka, Riwka and other synonyms of Rebecca.

Fainshtein, Isaak	Faynshteyn, Isya
Fainshtein, Isai	Faynshteyn, Iska
Fainshtein, Itzhak Yitzkhak	Faynshteyn, Izya
Fainstein, Ichak Yitzkhak	Faynshteyn, Itzkhok
Fainstein, Isac	Faynshteyn, Itzyk
Fainstian, Iczhack Yitzkhak	Faynshteyn, Ayzik
Fajnstajn, Icchak Yitzkhak	Faynshteyn, Isak
Fajnsztajn, Jcchak Yitzkhak	Faynshteyn, Itzkhok
Fajnsztein, Icek	Faynshteyn, Isaak
Faynshteyn, Isaak Isak	Faynshteyn, Itzkhak

Synonym indexes used in the Shoah Victims' Names Database at Yad Vashem.org show different variants of the given name Isaac. It also includes phonetic variants of Feinstein.

Fuzzy Searches. "Fuzzy" searches usually involve a set of complex rules that will identify a match if it is similar. Fuzzy search rules may accommodate transposition of letters, additional letters or missing letters. Few search engines offer this option. Fuzzy searches might consider the following names as identical: Mokotoff, Monkotoff, Motokoff.

Other Considerations

Websites in languages that use diacritical marks may require use of those marks in searches. Some Polish sites produce no results for Mokotow but find results for Mokotów. Sometimes a search yields too many hits, usually when dealing with an unusually large database. Fortunately, such databases tend to have sophisticated search engines; it is possible to look for options that permit qualifying a search according to age, birth year or record type. Avoid limiting the search based on attributes of the individual. Data such as birth year, age and place of birth may be inaccurate on a document, and names of spouses or parents may be spelled differently.

One-Name Research

Many Jewish genealogists claim that all persons with a given surname are related to each other. Consequently, when searching databases, a researcher may provide only the surname since he or she would consider any result to be an acceptable result.

The strategy for searching by surname only is different since the goal is to locate every record with that surname. Rather than search directly for the surname, first determine the capability of the search engine. Does it allow wildcards? Can it perform soundex or fuzzy searches? Does it require diacritical marks? Pick some common surname—Levi is a good choice—and examine the results. Since all persons in the world named Mokotoff are related to this author, when I search a new database I do one-name research, that is, I search for any record of a person named Mokotoff, Mokotow, Mokotov, Mokotowski, Mokotowicz, or any other spelling variant. If the search engine permits wild card searches, I search for Mokot*.

Sites in Non-native Languages

Use Google Translate (<translate.google.com>) to convert into your native language text on a website in a language you do not understand. The best browser to use for foreign languages is Google Chrome. It automatically detects if a website is not in the designated native language, indicates what it believes to be the language of the site and asks if the user wants the text translated. Unfortunately, an automatic translator can only translate text; it will not translate language embedded in graphic images. Often the name of the site is a graphic image—and the most important button on the search page, which says "Search," typically is a graphic image. Learn the word for "Search" in the languages you will need, for example, *rechercher* (French), *suche* (German), חיפוש (Hebrew), *szukaj* (Polish), ИСКАТЬ (Russian), *buscar* (Spanish).

Conclusion

Searching genealogical databases is not necessarily as simple as entering the information sought and examining the results. Errors in the database or its accompanying index may give false results, the worst example of which is the claim that a name is not present. Use of the techniques described above may locate many otherwise "missing" records.

Appendix B: Daitch-Mokotoff Soundex System

What can be more frustrating to a genealogist than to look through an alphabetical index of records and not find what is being sought and then find out later, perhaps years later, the data was there but with an alternate spelling? How do you locate towns of immigrant non-English-speaking ancestors when the only information available was passed down through the generations orally, and no matter how many spelling variants are tried, you cannot find the town on a map?

A major solution to these problems was provided 98 years ago when Robert C. Russell of Pittsburgh, Pennsylvania, was issued patent number 1,261,167 on April 2, 1918, for having "invented certain new and useful improvements in indexes...as will enable others skilled in the art to which it appertains to make and use the same." The idea of indexing information by how it sounds rather than alphabetically was born. It has become known as "soundexing."

A significant improvement to soundexing is the Daitch-Mokotoff Soundex System. In 1985, this author indexed the names of some 28,000 persons who legally changed their names while living in Palestine from 1921 to 1948, most of whom were Jews with Germanic or Slavic surnames. It was obvious there were numerous spelling variants of the same basic surname and the list should be soundexed. Using the Russell system, many Eastern European Jewish names which sound the same did not soundex the same. For example, names spelled interchangeably with the letter *w* or *v* (Moskowitz and Moskovitz) do not have the same soundex code in the Russell system. In collaboration with Randy Daitch, the author created the Daitch-Mokotoff Soundex System. The system is sometimes called the Jewish Soundex System and there are comments that it favors Germanic and Slavic names. This applies to the table only. If the table is changed to favor, as an example, Spanish names the D-M algorithm still would work successfully.

Daitch-Mokotoff Soundex System Rules

The rules for converting names into Daitch-Mokotoff code numbers are listed here. First turn briefly to the coding chart at the end of this appendix to familiarize yourself with the concept, and then return to the specific coding instructions on this page.

1. Surnames are translated into codes of six digits. Each sound in the name is assigned a number, as listed in the coding chart at the end of this appendix.

2. The letters A, E, I, O, U, J and Y are always coded at the beginning of a name, as in Ashkinaz (045640). In any other situation, they are ignored, except when two of these particular letters form a pair and the pair comes before a vowel, as in Maiorkis (619540), but not Fried (793000).

3. The letter H is coded at the beginning of a name, as in Halberstadt (587943) or preceding a vowel, as in Zamenhof (466570). Otherwise it is not coded.

4. When adjacent sounds combine to form a larger sound, they are given the code number of that larger sound, as in Miretsky, which is coded Miretsky (694500), rather than Mire-t-s-ky (693450).

5. When adjacent letters have the same code number, they are coded as one sound, as in Lassovsky, which is coded Lassovsky (847450), rather than La-s-sovsky (844745). When two identical letters or sounds are separated by a vowel, they are coded separately. Thus, Gandelman is coded Gandelman (563866), not Gandelman (563860).

6. When a name consists of more than one word, it is coded as if it were one word. For example, Ben David, which is treated as Bendavid (763730).

7. Several letters and letter combinations may produce more than one sound. The letter and letter combinations CH, CK, C, J and RZ are assigned two possible code numbers. Be sure to try both possibilities.

8. When a name lacks enough coded sounds to fill the six digits, the remaining digits are coded as zeroes, as in Romm (960000), which has only two sounds to be coded (R-M).

Examples:

Surnames	Alternate Spelling
F e i n s t ei n (764360)	F aj n sz t ej n (764360)
H i r s h f e l d (594783)	G e r s h f e l d (594783)
Ch a z a n o w (446700) or (546700)	K ha z a n o v (546700)

Daitch-Mokotoff Soundex Coding Chart

Letter	Alternate Spelling	Start of a Name	Before a Vowel	Any Other Situation
AI	AE, AJ, AO, AY	0	1	1
AU		0	7	1
A		0	N/C	N/C
B		7	7	7
CHS		5	54	54
CH	Try KH (5) and TCH (4)			
CK	Try K (5) and TSK (45)			
CZ	CS, CSZ, CZS	4	4	4
C	Try K (5) and TZ (4)			
DRZ	DRS	4	4	4
DS	DSH, DSZ	4	4	4
DZ	DZH, DZS	4	4	4
D	DT	3	3	3
EI	EA, EJ, EO, EY	0	1	1
EU		1	1	1
E		0	N/C	N/C
FB		7	7	7
F		7	7	7
G		5	5	5
H		5	5	N/C
IA	IE, IO, IU	1	N/C	N/C
I		0	N/C	N/C
J	Try Y (1) and DZH (4)			
KS		5	54	54
KH		5	5	5
K		5	5	5
L		8	8	8
MN			66	66
M		6	6	6
NM			66	66
N		6	6	6
OI	OA, OE, OJ, OU, OY	0	1	1
O		0	N/C	N/C
P	PF, PH	7	7	7
Q		5	5	5

N/C = not coded

Daitch-Mokotoff Soundex Coding Chart
(continued)

Letter	Alternate Spelling	Start of a Name	Before a Vowel	Any Other Situation
RZ, RS	Try RTZ (94) and ZH (4)			
R		9	9	9
SCHTSCH	SCHTSH, SCHTCH	2	4	4
SCH		4	4	4
SHTCH	SHCH, SHTSH	2	4	4
SHT	SCHT, SCHD	2	43	43
SH		4	4	4
STCH	STSCH, SC	2	4	4
STRZ	STRS, STSH	2	4	4
ST		2	43	43
SZCZ	SZCS	2	4	4
SZT	SHD, SZD, SD	2	43	43
SZ		4	4	4
S		4	4	4
TCH	TTCH, TTSCH	4	4	4
TH		3	3	3
TRZ	TRS	4	4	4
TSCH	TSH	4	4	4
S TTS	TTSZ, TC	4	4	4
TZ	TTZ, TZS, TSZ	4	4	4
T		3	3	3
UI	UA, UJ, UO, UY	0	1	1
U	UE	0	N/C	N/C
V		7	7	7
W		7	7	7
X		5	54	54
Y		1	N/C	N/C
ZDZ	ZDZH, ZHDZH	2	4	4
ZD	ZHD	2	43	43
ZH	ZS, ZSCH, ZSH	4	4	4
Z		4	4	4

N/C = not coded

Appendix C: Case Study– The Paternal History of Bernard Madoff

[This chapter originally was published in the Summer 2009 issue of AVOTAYNU: The International Review of Jewish Genealogy.]

Using the Internet and readily available resources, this author traced the family history of the notorious Bernie Madoff back five generations and confirmed that Madoff was not the family name when his ancestors arrived at Ellis Island. It is a classical example of a successful strategy to trace one's Eastern-European Jewish ancestry. It was all accomplished using only Internet resources.

Getting Started

Normally a beginner in family history research knows the names of his parents and grandparents, and possibly even great-grandparents. To determine the name of great-grandparents, if not known, one asks living parents, aunts or uncles for the names of their grandparents. In the case of Bernard Madoff, I learned his parents' names by Googling "Bernard Madoff parents." This yielded the information that "Bernard Madoff was born April 29, 1938, in New York City to parents Ralph and Sylvia Madoff." Knowing that his father's name was Ralph, I next consulted the 1930 United States census found at Ancestry.com. This invariably is my starting point in tracing a Jewish family history, because it includes a wealth of information that permits tracing the family back further generations.

Census Data

The 1930 census shows two Ralph Madoffs, one living in Akron, Ohio, born about 1919, and a second living in the Bronx, New York, born about 1911. Clearly, the Ralph in the Bronx is Madoff's father. The 1911 birth date also fits the profile of Madoff's father. It would mean he was 27 years old when Bernard was born. The other Ralph would have been only 19. A cautionary note: It is possible that neither is Madoff's father, because not every person was enumerated in the census, and his father might be a third Ralph Madoff.

The 1930 census revealed that Ralph was the son of David and Rose Madoff, both born in "Russia-Warsaw," and all of their children were born in Pennsylvania. David and Rose were both 48 years old; both were 23 years old when they got married. Both became naturalized citizens. Why did the census state that they were born in Russia when Warsaw is the capital of Poland? Poland did not appear on any map between 1795 and 1918. In 1795, in what was called the Third Partition of Poland, the superpowers of the day—Russia, Prussia and Austro-Hungary—

divided Poland among themselves, and Poland ceased to exist as an independent country. Only after World War I did Poland regain its autonomy. One of the chal-

The 1930 census is a good starting point, because it shows where people were born and when immigrants came to the U.S.

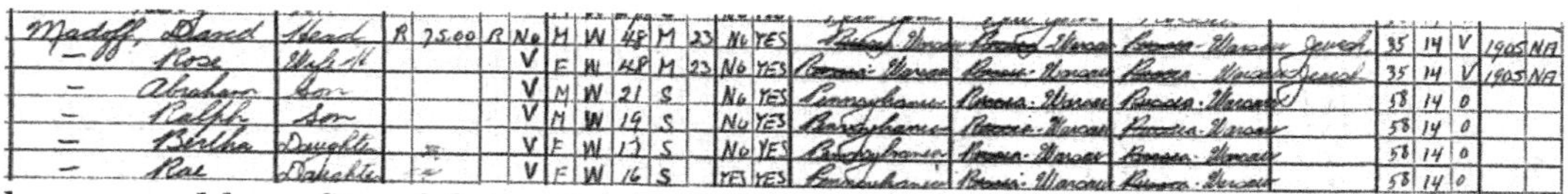

Madoff, David	Head	R	75.00	R	No	M	W	48	M	23	No	YES	[illegible]	[illegible]	[illegible]	Jewish	35	14	V	1905 NA
— Rose	Wife H				V	F	W	48	M	23	No	YES	[illegible]	[illegible]	[illegible]	Jewish	35	14	V	1905 NA
— Abraham	Son				V	M	W	21	S		No	YES	Pennsylvania	[illegible]	[illegible]		58	14	0	
— Ralph	Son				V	M	W	19	S		No	YES	Pennsylvania	[illegible]	[illegible]		58	14	0	
— Bertha	Daughter				V	F	W	17	S		No	YES	Pennsylvania	[illegible]	[illegible]		58	14	0	
— Rae	Daughter				V	F	W	16	S		YES	YES	Pennsylvania	[illegible]	[illegible]		58	14	0	

lenges and benefits of doing family history research is that you must learn about general history.

Census data often is highly unreliable, even though the sources of the information are the persons themselves. It is always wise to compare the information provided in other censuses, so my next step was to consult the 1920 and 1910 censuses at Ancestry.com.

The 1920 census shows David and Rose Madoff, both age 38, living in Scranton, Pennsylvania. David had arrived in the U.S. in 1908, and Rose's arrival year is shown as "unk[nown]." It indicated that David was naturalized in 1918. Searching the 1910 census for persons named Madoff living in Pennsylvania uncovers two families: one in Scranton, the other in Philadelphia. The 1910 census record for the Scranton Madoffs shows that David was not yet married and lived with his parents, Barnett and Annie, and six siblings. All arrived in the United States in 1908. David is listed as 25 years old (rather than the 28 years one would have expected if his age on the 1920 census were correct).

Finding the Passenger Arrival Record

Having gone back as far as possible in Madoff's family history within the United States, the problem was to find records of the family's presence in Europe. I was almost certain that the original name was not Madoff, but more likely a name beginning with M that was phonetically similar to Madoff. This was a common way Jewish immigrants Americanized their names. It was likely that David Madoff came through Ellis Island, but it also was possible that he entered the country through Philadelphia, since his final destination was Scranton, Penn-

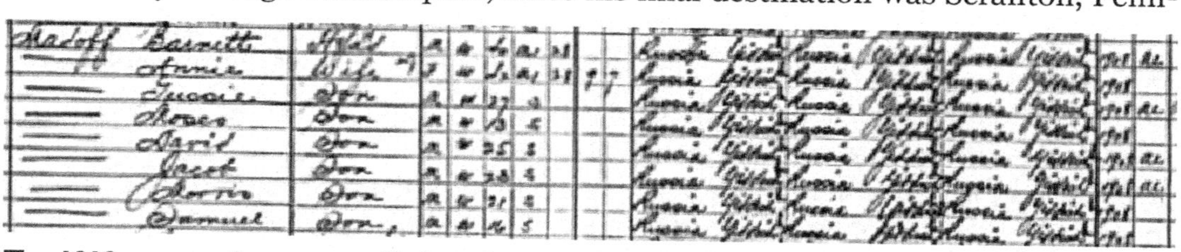

Madoff	Barnett	Head	[illegible]	Russia
—	Annie	Wife	[illegible]	Russia
—	[illegible]	Son	[illegible]	Russia
—	Moses	Son	[illegible]	Russia
—	David	Son	25	Russia
—	Jacob	Son	[illegible]	Russia
—	Morris	Son	[illegible]	Russia
—	Samuel	Son	[illegible]	Russia

The 1910 census shows grandfather, David, living with his parents. It states they arrived in the U.S. in 1908.

sylvania. Using the <stevemorse.org> site to search the Ellis Island database for any person whose given name started with "Da," whose last name started with M, who arrived in the U.S. between 1905 and 1909, who was born during the period 1883–1888 and who was a Jewish male produced no fruitful results.

Normally it is unwise to include any part of a given name, because the Eastern European Jewish immigrant typically arrived bearing his Yiddish name. A name as simple as Jacob may have been registered as Yankel, a Yiddish variant of Jacob. There are few variants of David other than Dave and Dawid; therefore, it seemed safe to include a portion of the given name. Despite trying many variants of the search, I failed to find the passenger manifest.

Another source likely to lead to the discovery of immigrant origins is naturalization documents. Searching Ancestry.com for David Madoff uncovered his naturalization documents from the U.S. Circuit and District Courts for the Middle District of Pennsylvania—with a treasure trove of information. David Solomon Madoff, born on December 13, 1883, in Pshedborsh, Poland, came to the U.S. on May 11, 1907, on the *Graf Waldersee* and declared his intention to become a citizen in Scranton on December 7, 1909.

Personal experience has demonstrated that naturalization records are notoriously inaccurate sources of arrival date, ship's name and town of birth. If a citizen applied for naturalization many years after arrival, he often could not remember the name of the ship and certainly not the exact date of arrival. Place of birth often was written phonetically by the clerk taking the information verbally. It is

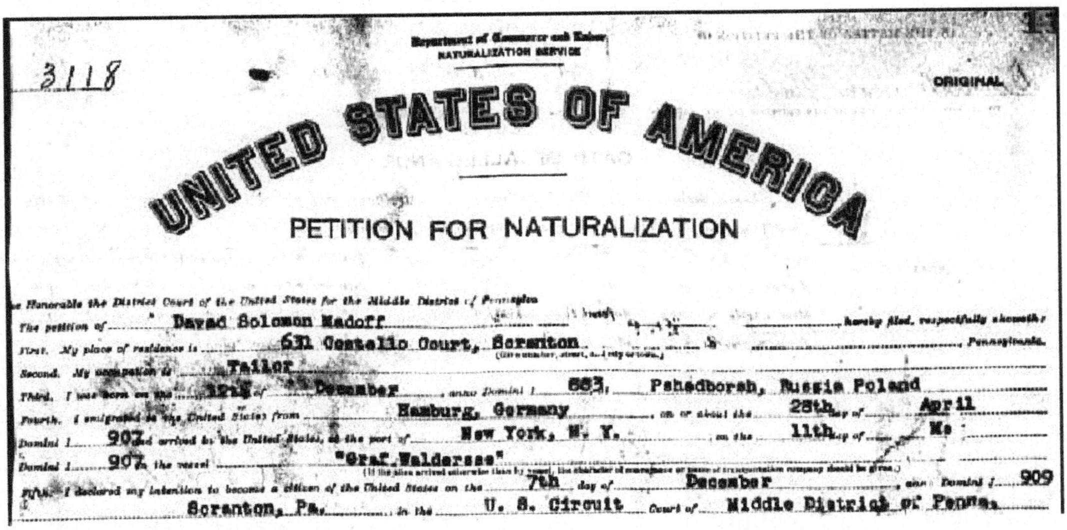

Department of Commerce and Labor
NATURALIZATION SERVICE

3118

ORIGINAL

UNITED STATES OF AMERICA

PETITION FOR NATURALIZATION

...e Honorable the District Court of the United States for the Middle District of Pennsylvania
The petition of Davad Solomon Madoff hereby filed, respectfully showeth:
First. My place of residence is 631 Costello Court, Scranton Pennsylvania.
Second. My occupation is Tailor
Third. I was born on the 13th of December anno Domini 1883, Pshedborsh, Russia Poland
Fourth. I emigrated to the United States from Hamburg, Germany on or about the 28th day of April
anno Domini 1907 and arrived in the United States, at the port of New York, N. Y. on the 11th day of May
anno Domini 1907 in the vessel "Graf Waldersee"
Fifth. I declared my intention to become a citizen of the United States on the 7th day of December anno Domini 1909
Scranton, Pa. in the U. S. Circuit Court of Middle District of Penna.

When an immigrant changed his name after coming to the U.S. and the name in the Old Country is not known, naturalization records will show the ship on which he arrived. Going through the passenger list, a researcher usually will find the former name.

useful to confirm that the named ship did arrive on the named date. Use the "Ellis Island Ship Lists (1892–1957)" function at the Morse site. It demonstrated that, indeed, the *Graf Waldersee* arrived on May 11, 1907, in New York from Hamburg.

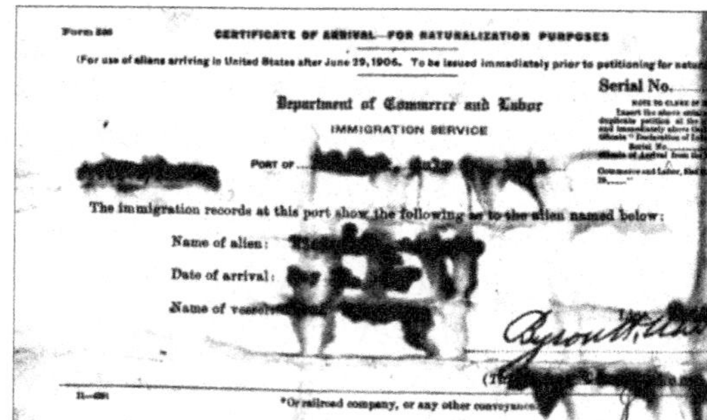
Form 380

CERTIFICATE OF ARRIVAL—FOR NATURALIZATION PURPOSES

(For use of aliens arriving in United States after June 29, 1906. To be issued immediately prior to petitioning for natu...

Serial No.

Department of Commerce and Labor

IMMIGRATION SERVICE

PORT OF ...

The immigration records at this port show the following ... alien named below:

Name of alien:

Date of arrival:

Name of vessel:

*Or railroad company, or any other conveyance

A good source to determine the surname of an immigrant is the Certificate of Arrival attached to the naturalization papers. Starting with immigrants who arrived after June 26, 1906, the U.S. required verification that the person arrived legally. The name was searched in the passenger manifest, and the information was copied from the manifest, including the name at time of arrival. Unfortunately, the certificate for Solomon David Madoff (above) was water damaged obliterating the name. The author hired a researcher to get a better copy of the naturalization records at the Family History Library in Salt Lake City. Included on the microfilm was a retyped certificate of arrival showing the immigrant's name was Miodownik (below).

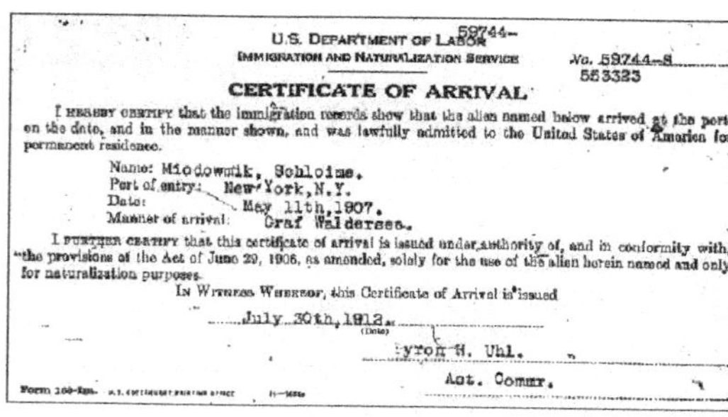
U.S. DEPARTMENT OF LABOR 59744-

IMMIGRATION AND NATURALIZATION SERVICE

No. 59744-8

553323

CERTIFICATE OF ARRIVAL

I HEREBY CERTIFY that the immigration records show that the alien named below arrived at the port, on the date, and in the manner shown, and was lawfully admitted to the United States of America for permanent residence.

Name: Miodownik, Schloime.

Port of entry: New York, N.Y.

Date: May 11th, 1907.

Manner of arrival: Graf Waldersee.

I FURTHER CERTIFY that this certificate of arrival is issued under authority of, and in conformity with, the provisions of the Act of June 29, 1906, as amended, solely for the use of the alien herein named and only for naturalization purposes.

IN WITNESS WHEREOF, this Certificate of Arrival is issued

July 30th, 1912.

(Date)

Byron H. Uhl.

Act. Commr.

Form 160

At worst, every page of the ship's manifest could be searched looking for a male Jew (Race: Hebrew on the document) about 22 years old who met the profile of David Madoff. Rather than search every page of the manifest, I took a shortcut and used Ancestry.com's Ellis Island database where I found the correct entry after about an hour by searching the ship for any person named either David or Dawid. Starting with the naturalization record, I recalled that most Jewish men born in the 19th century had two given names—in this case, David Solomon. The first given name was his religious name, known as his *shem kodesh*. The second name was his everyday name, known as his *kinnui*. Perhaps Madoff came to the U.S. as Solomon. The problem is that the Americanized name Solomon has many Yiddish variants, including Shlomo, Shloime and Shlome. He could have arrived with the Polish spelling, Szlama. Most likely, since he had left via Hamburg, his name would have been recorded with the German spelling of Schlame or Schloime. But a search of New York arrivals on Ancestry.com for Sch* arriving on the *Graf Waldersee* in 1907 yielded nothing.

Because David Solomon Madoff had left Europe via the port of Hamburg, I tried the Hamburg emigration lists on Ancestry.com and found him—Schloma Miadownik. Why couldn't he be found in the Ellis Island list on Ancestry.com? In that database, he was indexed as Saloma Miodowink [sic]. On the Ellis Island record, he is listed as Schlame Miadownik. The person extracting the record for Ancestry.com did not read the record properly. So, it appeared, the Miadownik family Americanized their name to Madoff.

Veteran genealogists will tell you that once you solve a difficult problem and know the answer, you realize that there could have been a shorter way to do the research. In this case, the record could have been solved in less than two minutes by searching <stevemorse.org> for any Jewish male whose last name started with M and who arrived on the *Graf Waldersee* on May 11, 1907. The entry in the Ellis Island Database is for Haloma [sic] Miodownik.

What proof do we have that the person found actually was David Solomon Madoff? The passenger record states that he was going to Scranton, Pennsylvania. He was with his wife, Reisel, and eldest daughter, Schewe, aged 10 months. Schewe's fate is unknown; she does not appear in the 1920 census.

Crossing the Pond

Armed with the original surname and the information that David was born in Pshedborsh, it was now possible to use other Internet resources to trace the Madoff/Miodownik family history. Curious about the origin of the name Miodownik, I consulted Alexander Beider's *A Dictionary of Jewish Surnames from the Kingdom of Poland.* Beider states that the origin of the name is either from the Polish word for "honey cake" or from the root surname Miod, which is the Polish word for "honey." Since Jews in that area did not acquire hereditary surnames until the beginning of the 19th century, Beider suggests that the progenitor of the Madoff name may have been in the honey business.

As coauthor of *Where Once We Walked* (WOWW), a gazetteer of some 23,500 towns in Europe where Jews lived before the Holocaust, I instantly realized that Pshedborsh actually is Przedborz, Poland. Other researchers could have used the Daitch-Mokotoff Soundex Index in the book to confirm the locality. Pshedborsh soundexes to 743794; the only entry in the index under that code number is for Przedborz.

Focus now turned to the Jewish Records Indexing-Poland project on the Internet at <www.jri-poland.org>. The database is housed on <JewishGen.org> and can be accessed from its home page as well. Doing a soundex search for Miodownik produced nearly 1,000 hits throughout Poland—understandable, given that the etymology of the name related to someone in the honey business. JewishGen separates the list by the old czarist provinces (*guberniyas*); Przedborz was in Radom guberniya, which yielded only 17 hits for Miodownik. The JRI-Poland index for Przedborz shows the birth of Szljana [sic] Dawid Miodownik in 1882, undoubtedly David Solomon Madoff. In the neighboring town of Radoszyce,

Radoszyce M1826-59,66-84
Radom Gubernia / Kielce Province
Located at 51°05' 20°14'
Last updated January 2001

Surname	Givenname	Year	Type	Akt	Status	Film
KIENBAM?	Liba	1850	M	6		719333
MIODOWNIK	Izrael	1850	M	6		719333
MIODOWNIK	Szaja	1855	M	4		719334
MLYNSKA	Ruchla	1855	M	4		719334
FRIDLEWSKA	Haia? Rywka	1879	M	4		1809027
MIODOWNIKI	Berek	1879	M	4		1809027

Przedborz M1823-29,32-46,79-86 BD 1879-86
Radom Gubernia / Kielce Province
Located at 51°05' 19°53'
Last updated November 2000

Surname	Givenname	Year	Type	Akt	Town	Film
MODOWNIK	Szljana Dawid	1882	B	4		
MEDOWNIK	Jakub Jusek	1884	B	21		
MEDOWNIK	Rela	1885	B	149		
MEDOWNIK	Jankel	1885	M	27		

JRI–Poland project has an index to the birth of Solomon David Miodownik and the marriage of his parents, Haia Rywka Fridleweska and Berek Miodownik. The marriage records would show the names of parents taking the Madoff ancestry one more generation.

the index shows, the marriage took place in 1879 of Berek Miodowniki to Haia Rivka Fridelewska, undoubtedly David's parents, Barnett and Annie.

Microfilm copies of both the birth and the marriage record are held in the LDS (Mormon) Family History Library in Salt Lake City. On my next research trip to Salt Lake City, I plan to make copies of these records. Alternately, I could request that the microfilms be sent to a local Family History Center where I could view them and make copies. The marriage record of Barnett Madoff will give me the names of his parents. If he did not come from Radoszyce, which is likely, the record may show the town of his birth; that in turn will permit tracing the Madoff family back additional generations. I already know that Barnett's mother's name was Golda, because his Ellis Island record was found. He came as Berl (a variant of Berek) and indicated that the closest person in the country from which he had come was his mother, Golda.

Networking

Make people aware of what you are researching, because they may have information valuable to your efforts. This case study was originally published in the Summer 2009 issue of AVOTAYNU. It was read by Warren Blatt, managing director of JewishGen. He sent me the following e-mail:

> Using the back issues of the *Kielce-Radom SIG Journal*, I was able to go back another few generations:
>
> Berek MIODOWNIKI m. 1879 in Radoszyce [Radoszyce 1879 M#4], age 19 parents: Szlama (deceased) & Sora Golda b. 1860 in Lopuszno [Malogoszcz 1860 B#7] parents: Szlama, age 20 & Sora Golda, age 20
>
> Szlama Dawid MIODOWNIKI m. 1859 in Malogoszcz [Malogoszcz 1859 M#4], age 18 parents: Mosiek & Gitla
>
> bride: Sara Golda HARENDORF, age 19, dau of Herszel & Ruchla b. 1840 in Lopuszno [Malagoszcz 1840 B#20]
>
> parents: Mosiek (day-laborer, age 36) & Gitla (age 40)
>
> Mosiek MIODOWNIKI m. 1837 in Malogoszcz [Malogoszcz 1837 M #3], widower, age 28 parents: Leybus & Czarna, of Lopuszno & Checiny bride: Gitla ALEXANDROWICZ, widow, age 40, of Lopuszno dau of Jankel & Rochla Moszkowna
>
> So Mosiek MIODOWNIKI was born circa 1809, the son of Leybus and Czarna.
>
> There are many other entries for MIODOWNIKI siblings and cousins, as well as the maternal lines (FRYDLEWSKI, MIODECKI, HARENDORF) in the extracts of Radoszyce, Malogoszcz, and surrounding towns.

Accuracy of Research

Is this compiled ancestry of Bernard Madoff's accurate? There is an element of doubt. The weakest link is the fact that two David Madoffs are recorded. The one I believe to be the correct David Madoff came to the United States with a wife and child, yet the only David Madoff that fits Bernard's David Madoff is the one listed in the census as single and living with his parents. I found other records on Ancestry.com for David Solomon Madoff. His World War I draft registration showed his residence in Scranton and his birth date as March 15, 1882. His World War II (Old Men's) draft registration shows him living in Brooklyn, New York, with a stated birth date of March 18, 1890. In his naturalization records, he stated that he was born on December 12, 1893. Only by reading his birth record from the 1882 birth register of the Jews of Przedborz will the correct date be found.

In spite of these discrepancies, the thread of evidence is clear. Ralph Madoff is found in the 1920 census with brother and sister, Abraham and Bertha. David Solomon Madoff's naturalization record lists his children as Abraham Zooken (Ralph) and Brucha (Bertha). David registered for the World War I draft as David Solomon Madoff in Scranton. The absolute proof would be the birth record of Szlama Miodownik at the Family History Library showing that his parents were Berek and Chaia Rivka.

Paternal Ancestry of Bernard Madoff

Bernard Madoff 1938–
 Ralph Madoff 1910–1972
  David Solomon Madoff (Szlama Dawid Miodownik) 1882–
   Barnett Madoff (Berek Miodownik) 1860–?
    Szlama Dawid Miodownik 1841–?
     Mosiek Miodownik 1809–?
      Leybus Miodownik bef 1790–?

Conclusion

The Madoff family research relied on the tools typically used when beginning to trace a Jewish-American family whose ancestors came from Eastern Europe—all of which are available on the web. Start with the 1930 census to gather basic facts. If the family arrived before 1920, include the 1920 census. Look at all census records as far back in time as possible. Then look for the family's arrival at the Port of New York using the <Stevemorse.org> website. Depending on the year of arrival, the record may supply the name of the last place of residence and/or place of birth. Next, go to JewishGen and use its vast resources, organized by contemporary country, to locate records of earlier ancestors.

Illustrations

RZECZPOSPOLITA POLSKA

URZĄD STANU CYWILNEGO w Sosnowcu--------------

Województwo katowickie-------------------------

Odpis skrócony aktu urodzenia

1. Nazwisko Wajngarten-------------------------
2. Imię (imiona) Szyja-----------------------
3. Data urodzenia pietnastego lipca tysiac dziewiećset dziesiatego (15.7.1910) roku---
4. Miejsce urodzenia Sosnowiec------------------
5. Imię i nazwisko rodowe (ojca) Moszek Wajngarten---------
6 Imię i nazwisko rodowe (matki) Frajda Ruchla Koniecpolska-

Poświadcza się zgodność powyższego odpisu z treścią aktu urodzenia Nr 167/27/12

Sosnowiec, data 1994.02.23

Miejsce na opłatę skarbową

URZĄD STANU CYWILNEGO W SOSNOWCU

m.p.

KIEROWNIK Urzędu Stanu Cywilnego

mgr inż. Arkadiusz Trzuskowski

Birth Record: Transcript of a Polish birth record obtained from the civil registration office of Sosnowiec, Poland. It is the record of the birth of Szyja (Joshua) Wajngarten, son of Moszek (Moses) Wajngarten and Frajda Ruchla (Frieda Rachel) Koniecpolska. Transcripts are not as valuable as original records because of the risk of transcription error; original records often have additional valuable information.

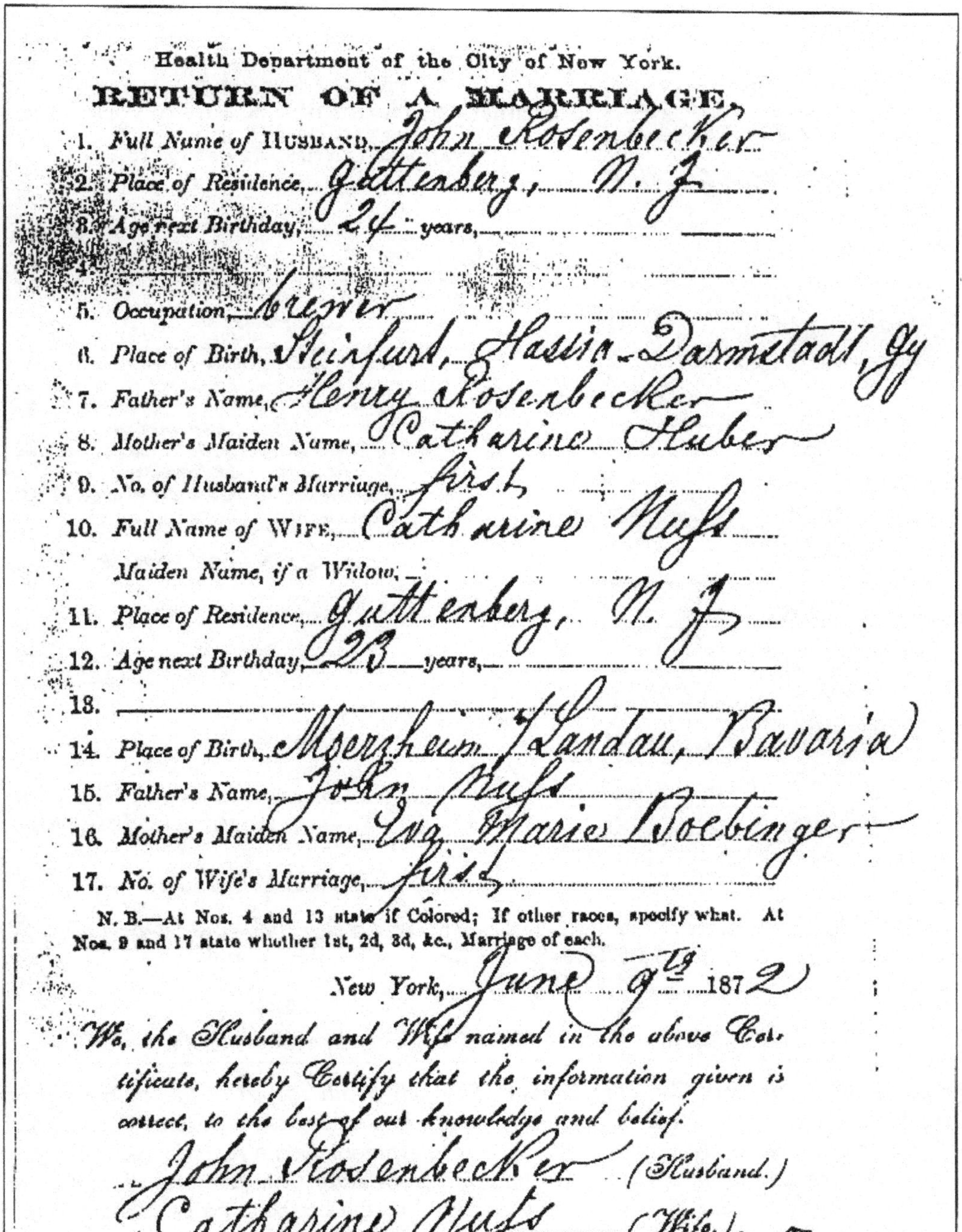

Health Department of the City of New York.

RETURN OF A MARRIAGE.

1. *Full Name of* HUSBAND, John Rosenbecker
2. *Place of Residence*, Guttenberg, N. J.
3. *Age next Birthday*, 24 years,
4.
5. *Occupation*, brewer
6. *Place of Birth*, Steinfurt, Hessia-Darmstadt, Gy
7. *Father's Name*, Henry Rosenbecker
8. *Mother's Maiden Name*, Catharine Huber
9. *No. of Husband's Marriage*, first
10. *Full Name of* WIFE, Catharine Nuss

    Maiden Name, if a Widow, –
11. *Place of Residence*, Guttenberg, N. J.
12. *Age next Birthday* 23 years,
13.
14. *Place of Birth*, Moerzheim, Landau, Bavaria
15. *Father's Name*, John Nuss
16. *Mother's Maiden Name*, Eva Marie Boebinger
17. *No. of Wife's Marriage*, first

N. B.—At Nos. 4 and 13 state if Colored; If other races, specify what. At Nos. 9 and 17 state whether 1st, 2d, 3d, &c., Marriage of each.

New York, June 9th 1872

We, the Husband and Wife named in the above Certificate, hereby Certify that the information given is correct, to the best of our knowledge and belief.

John Rosenbecker (*Husband.*)

Catharine Nuss (*Wife.*)

Marriage Record: *This 1872 New York City marriage record includes the ages of the bride and groom; places of birth in Germany; and names of parents, including maiden names of mothers.*

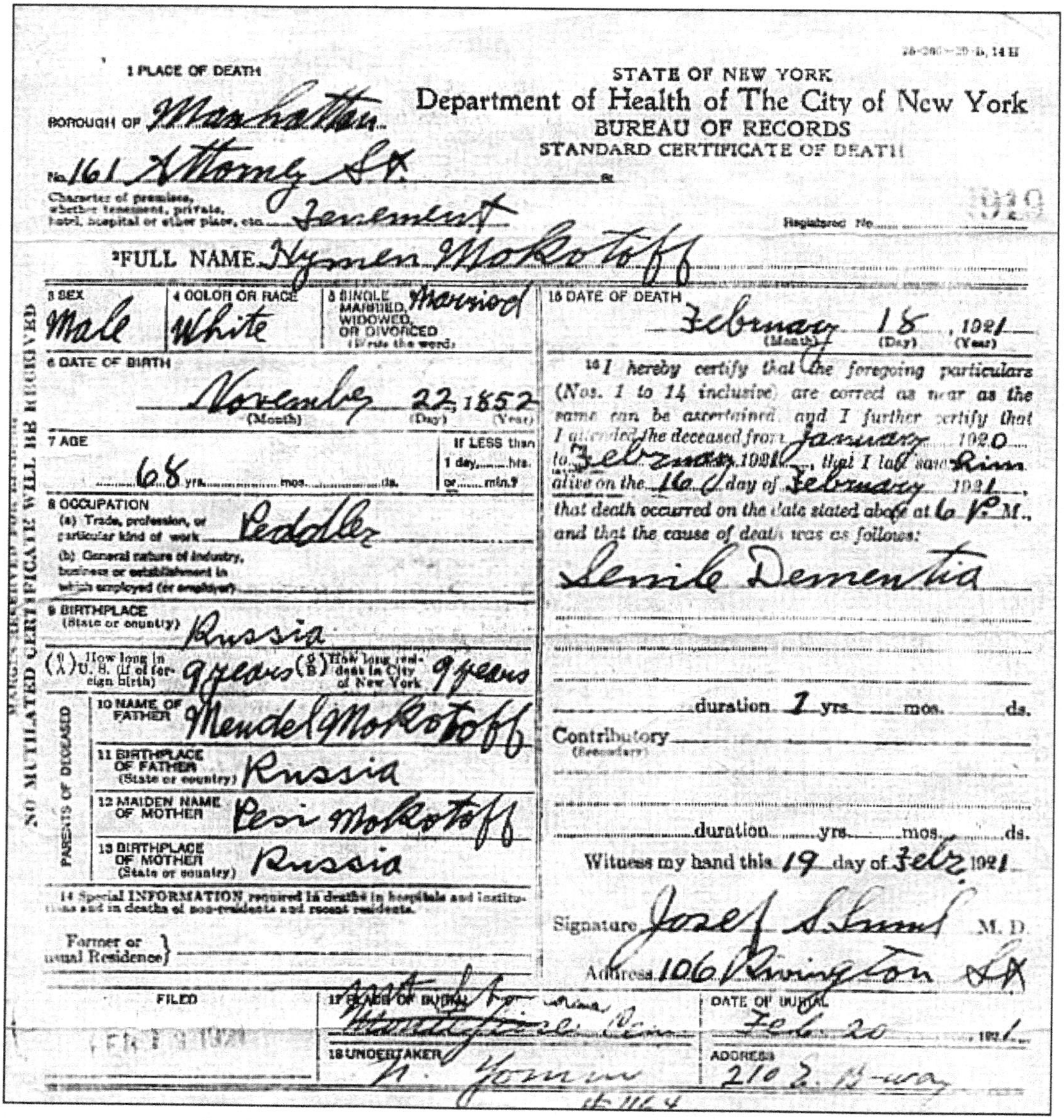

STATE OF NEW YORK
Department of Health of The City of New York
BUREAU OF RECORDS
STANDARD CERTIFICATE OF DEATH

1 PLACE OF DEATH
BOROUGH OF Manhattan
No. 161 Attorney St.
Character of premises, whether tenement, private, hotel, hospital or other place, etc. Tenement
Registered No.

2 FULL NAME Hymen Mokotoff

3 SEX: Male	4 COLOR OR RACE: White
5 SINGLE, MARRIED, WIDOWED OR DIVORCED (Write the word): Married	15 DATE OF DEATH: February 18, 1921 (Month) (Day) (Year)
6 DATE OF BIRTH: November 22, 1852 (Month) (Day) (Year)	
7 AGE: 68 yrs. ... mos. ... ds. If LESS than 1 day, ... hrs. or ... min.?	
8 OCCUPATION (a) Trade, profession, or particular kind of work: Peddler	
(b) General nature of industry, business or establishment in which employed (or employer)	
9 BIRTHPLACE (State or country): Russia	
(A) How long in U.S. (if of foreign birth): 9 years	(B) How long resident in City of New York: 9 years
10 NAME OF FATHER: Mendel Mokotoff	
11 BIRTHPLACE OF FATHER (State or country): Russia	
12 MAIDEN NAME OF MOTHER: Pesi Mokotoff	
13 BIRTHPLACE OF MOTHER (State or country): Russia	

16 I hereby certify that the foregoing particulars (Nos. 1 to 14 inclusive) are correct as near as the same can be ascertained, and I further certify that I attended the deceased from January 1920 to February 1921, that I last saw him alive on the 16 day of February 1921, that death occurred on the date stated above at 6 P.M., and that the cause of death was as follows:

Senile Dementia

duration 1 yrs. ... mos. ... ds.

Contributory (Secondary)

duration ... yrs. ... mos. ... ds.

Witness my hand this 19 day of Feb 1921

Signature Josef S. ... M.D.

Address 106 Rivington St.

14 Special INFORMATION required in deaths in hospitals and institutions and in deaths of non-residents and recent residents.

Former or usual Residence

FILED

17 PLACE OF BURIAL: ... Montefiore Cem.

DATE OF BURIAL: Feb. 20, 1921

18 UNDERTAKER: N. Yomm...

ADDRESS: 210 E. B-way

Death Record: *New York City Department of Health death record of the author's great-grandfather, Hyman Mokotoff. It provides his birth date, occupation, parents' names, number of years in U.S. and New York City, place of internment. Death records frequently have errors since the informant only has second-hand knowledge. The date of birth is incorrect (although it may be what the decedent thought). Also the mother's name is inaccurate. It may represent the last wife of the father, Menachem Mendel.*

Surname	Given Name	Age	Month	Day	Year	Certificate Number	County	Born
Silverstein	Hyman	61 y	July	16	1937	15679	Kings	1875 - 1876
Silverstein	Hyman	54 y	Jul	22	1921	4304	Bronx	1866 - 1867
Silverstein	Hyman	41 y	Jan	29	1947	2412	Kings	1905 - 1906
Silverstein	Hyman	77 y	Jan	21	1941	800	Bronx	1863 - 1864
Silverstein	Hyman	55 y	Dec	17	1937	26922	Manhattan	1881 - 1882
Silverstein	Hyman	41 y	Apr	28	1929	10567	Kings	1887 - 1888
Silverstein	Hyman	56 y	Jan	28	1925	2244	Kings	1868 - 1869
Silverstein	Hyman	78 y	Apr	23	1939	9476	Kings	1860 - 1861
Silverstein	Hyman	65 y	Aug	5	1923	5240	Bronx	1857 - 1858
Silverstein	Hyman	61 y	Jan	20	1947	1702	Kings	1885 - 1886
Silverstein	Hyman	70 y	Oct	11	1919	20362	Kings	1848 - 1849
Silverstein	Hyman	53 y	June	22	1938	13384	Manhattan	1884 - 1885
Silverstein	Hyman	50 y	Nov	11	1929	22668	Kings	1878 - 1879

Death Index: *Results of searching for Hyman Silverstein in the death index for New York City found at ItalianGen.org. Vital record indexes for many U.S. cities exist on the Internet.*

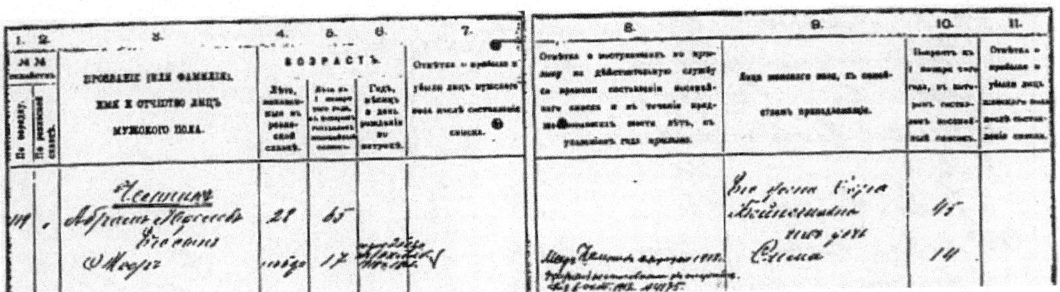

Russian Census: *Excerpt from a list of families of Jalowka, Poland, in 1910 shows the family of Abram Yudelev Chemnik, age 65; his son, Meir, age 17; wife, Sora Beineshevna, age 45; and daughter, Sima, age 14. Men are shown on the left side of the page and women on the right. At the time, Jalowka was in the Russian Empire and the document was written in Cyrillic. Russian given names include a patronymic. Thus, we know that Abram's father's name was Yudel and Sora's father was Beinish. Sima immigrated to the U.S. in 1914. Meir remained in Poland and was a Holocaust victim. The eldest daughter, Frusha, is the author's maternal grandmother. She has immigrated to the U.S. in 1905 before the census was taken.*

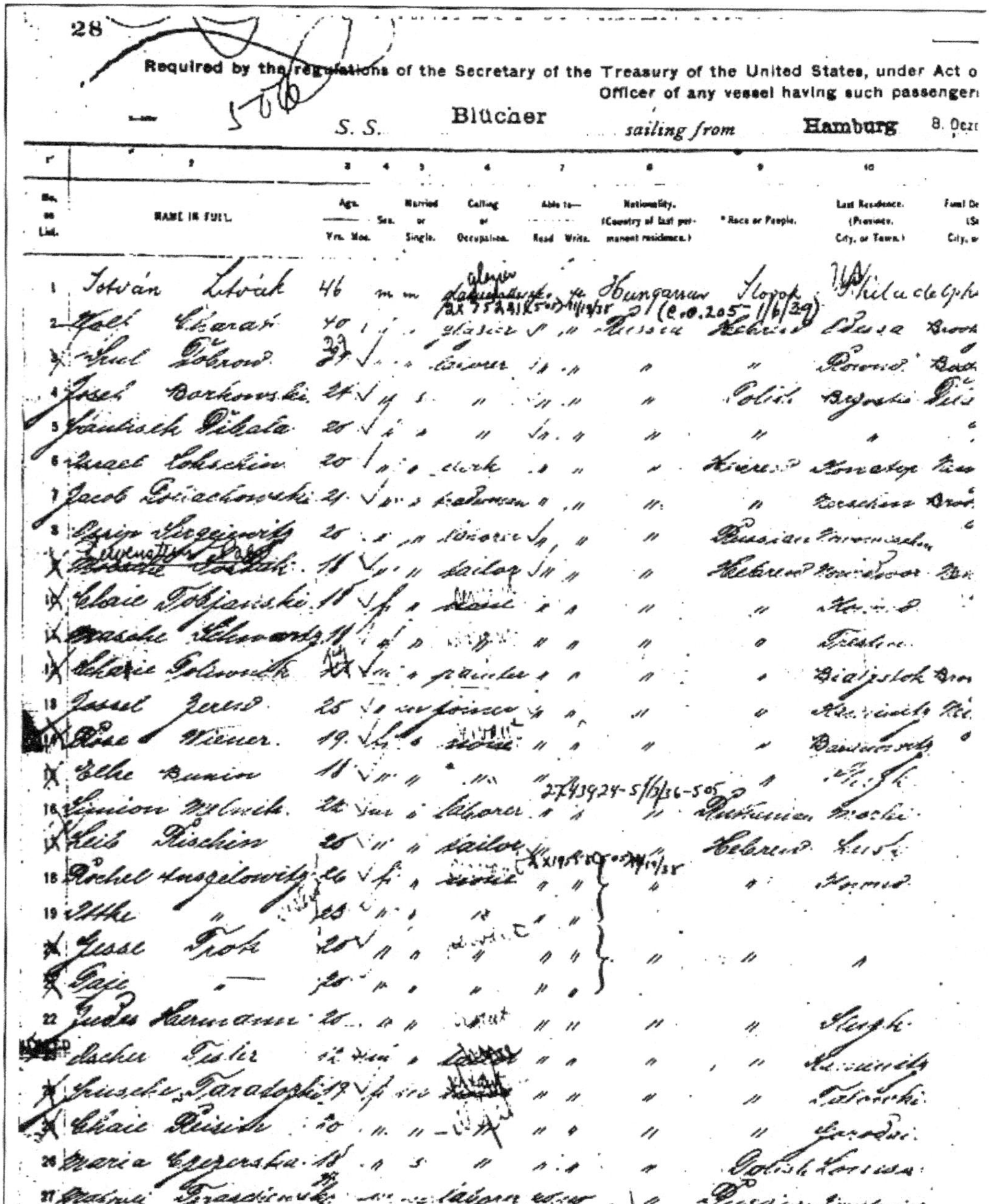
28

Required by the regulations of the Secretary of the Treasury of the United States, under Act o
Officer of any vessel having such passenger

S. S. Blücher sailing from Hamburg 8. Dez

No. on List.	NAME IN FULL.	Age. Yrs. Mos.	Sex.	Married or Single.	Calling or Occupation.	Able to— Read Write.	Nationality. (Country of last permanent residence.)	* Race or People.	Last Residence. (Province, City, or Town.)	Final De (St City, o
1	2	3	4	5	6	7	8	9	10	

Passenger Arrival Record: *(left and right pages) A 1907 ship's manifest showing much information including age, race (Hebrew for Jews), last residence, and name and address where immigrant was going. Line 24 shows the author's maternal grandmother written as Frushe Taratozski. Column 10 states that the her last residence was Jalowka.*

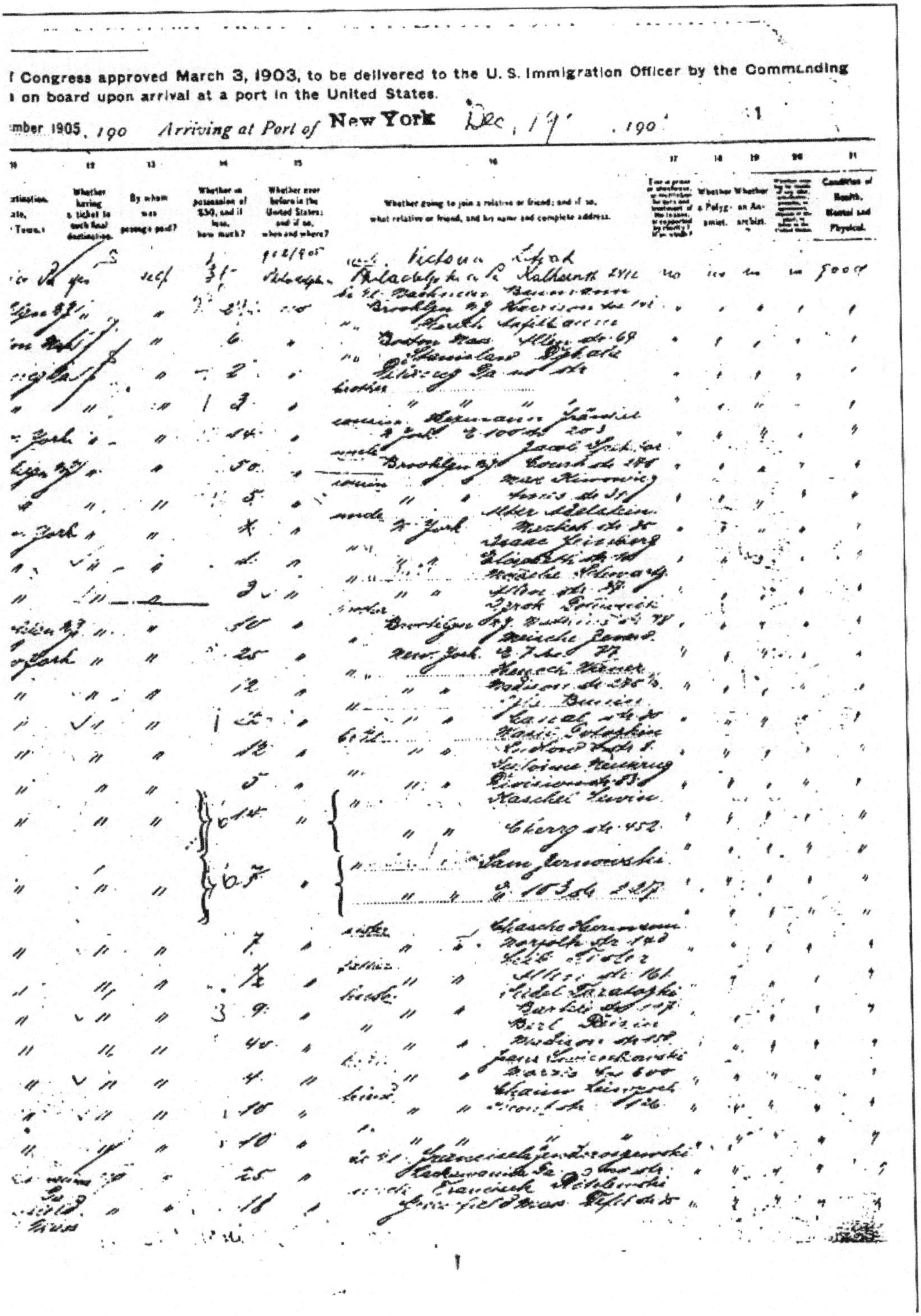

f Congress approved March 3, 1903, to be delivered to the U. S. Immigration Officer by the Commanding
on board upon arrival at a port in the United States.

mber 1905, *190* *Arriving at Port of* New York *Dec. 19* , *190*

…stination. …ate, …Town.	Whether having a ticket to such final destination.	By whom was passage paid?	Whether in possession of $50, and if less, how much?	Whether ever before in the United States; and if so, when and where?	Whether going to join a relative or friend; and if so, what relative or friend, and his name and complete address.		Whether a Polygamist.	Whether an Anarchist.		Condition of Health, Mental and Physical.

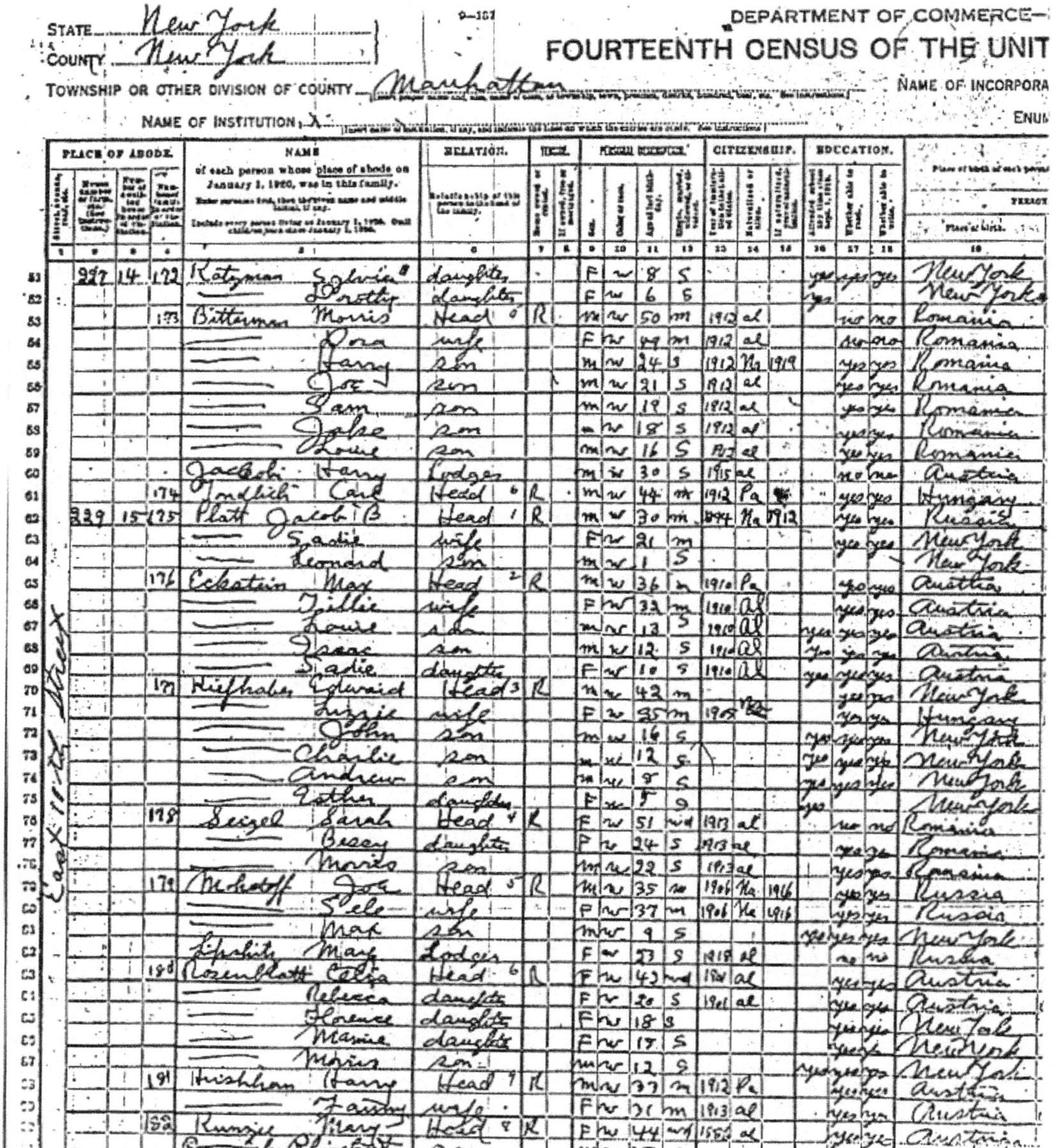

STATE New York
COUNTY New York
TOWNSHIP OR OTHER DIVISION OF COUNTY Manhattan
NAME OF INSTITUTION X

DEPARTMENT OF COMMERCE—
FOURTEENTH CENSUS OF THE UNIT
NAME OF INCORPORA
ENUM

Street: East 11?th Street

Line	House number	Dwelling	Family	Name	Relation	Home owned or rented	Sex	Color	Age	Marital	Year of immigration	Naturalized or alien	Year of naturalization	Attended school	Able to read	Able to write	Place of birth
51	227	14	172	Katzman Sylvia	daughter		F	w	8	S				yes	yes	yes	New York
52				— Dorothy	daughter		F	w	6	S				yes			New York
53			173	Bitterman Morris	Head	R	m	w	50	m	1912	al			no	no	Romania
54				— Rosa	wife		F	w	49	m	1912	al			no	no	Romania
55				— Harry	son		m	w	24	s	1912	Na	1919		yes	yes	Romania
56				— Joe	son		m	w	21	s	1912	al			yes	yes	Romania
57				— Sam	son		m	w	19	s	1912	al			yes	yes	Romania
58				— Jake	son		m	w	18	s	1912	al			yes	yes	Romania
59				— Louie	son		m	w	16	S	1912	al			yes	yes	Romania
60				Jacobi Harry	Lodger		m	w	30	s	1915	al			no	no	Austria
61			174	Gondlich Carl	Head	R	m	w	44	m	1912	Pa			yes	yes	Hungary
62	229	15	175	Platt Jacob B	Head	R	m	w	30	m	1894	Na	1912		yes	yes	Russia
63				— Sadie	wife		F	w	21	m					yes	yes	New York
64				— Leonard	son		m	w	1	S							New York
65			176	Eckstein Max	Head	R	m	w	36	m	1910	Pa			yes	yes	Austria
66				— Tillie	wife		F	w	32	m	1910	Al			yes	yes	Austria
67				— Louie	son		m	w	13	S	1910	Al		yes	yes	yes	Austria
68				— Isaac	son		m	w	12	S	1910	Al		yes	yes	yes	Austria
69				— Sadie	daughter		F	w	10	S	1910	Al		yes	yes	yes	Austria
70			177	Kiefhaber Edward	Head	R	m	w	42	m					yes	yes	New York
71				— Lizzie	wife		F	w	35	m	1905	Na			yes	yes	Hungary
72				— John	son		m	w	16	s				yes	yes	yes	New York
73				— Charlie	son		m	w	12	s				yes	yes	yes	New York
74				— Andrew	son		m	w	8	s				yes	yes	yes	New York
75				— Esther	daughter		F	w	5	s				yes			New York
76			178	Seigel Sarah	Head	R	F	w	51	wd	1913	al			no	no	Romania
77				— Bessy	daughter		F	w	24	s	1913	al			yes	yes	Romania
78				— Morris	son		m	w	22	s	1913	al			yes	yes	Romania
79			179	Mokotoff Joe	Head	R	m	w	35	m	1906	Na	1916		yes	yes	Russia
80				— Sele	wife		F	w	37	m	1906	Na	1916		yes	yes	Russia
81				— Max	son		m	w	9	s				yes	yes	yes	New York
82				Lipshitz May	Lodger		F	w	23	s	1918	al			no	no	Russia
83			180	Rozenblatt Celia	Head	R	F	w	43	wd	1901	al			yes	yes	Austria
84				— Rebecca	daughter		F	w	20	s	1901	al			yes	yes	Austria
85				— Florence	daughter		F	w	18	s					yes	yes	New York
86				— Marie	daughter		F	w	17	s					yes	yes	New York
87				— Morris	son		m	w	12	s				yes	yes	yes	New York
88			181	Hirshhorn Harry	Head	R	m	w	37	m	1912	Pa			yes	yes	Austria
89				— Fanny	wife		F	w	31	m	1913	al			yes	yes	Austria
90			182	Runzie Mary	Head	R	F	w	44	wd	1886	al			yes	yes	Austria
				Rhinehart	son		m	w	15	s							

Census Record: *The 1920 New York City census contains valuable information about citizenship, including year of immigration; whether naturalized or alien; and, if naturalized, year of naturalization. Line 79 shows the household of the author's great-uncle, Joe Mokotoff, with his wife, Sele, and son, Max.*

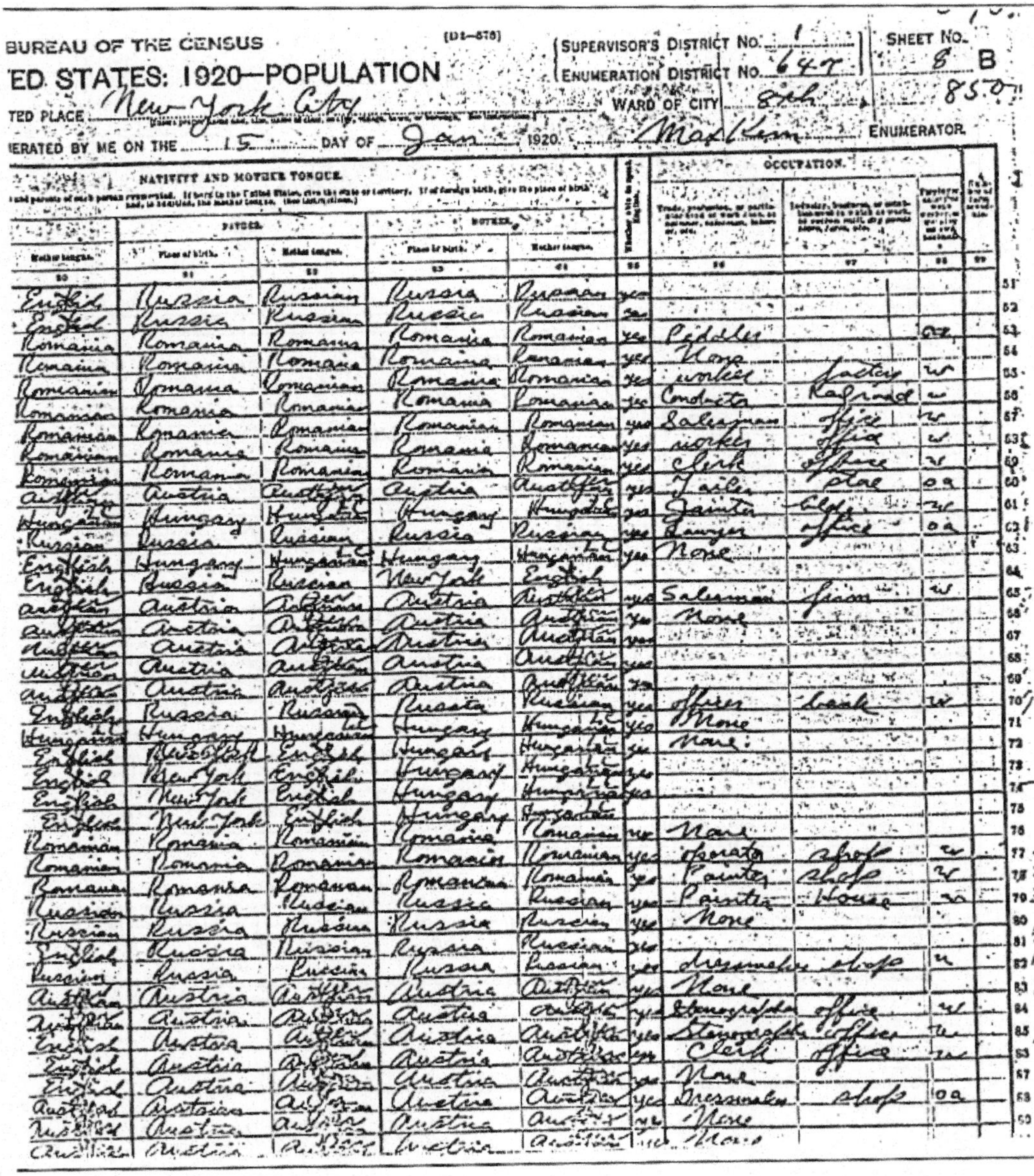

BUREAU OF THE CENSUS (D1—878)

ED STATES: 1920—POPULATION

SUPERVISOR'S DISTRICT NO. 1
ENUMERATION DISTRICT NO. 647
SHEET NO. 8 B
850

TED PLACE New York City
WARD OF CITY 8th

ERATED BY ME ON THE 15 DAY OF Jan 1920. Max Klein ENUMERATOR.

NATIVITY AND MOTHER TONGUE.

Mother tongue	Father: Place of birth	Father: Mother tongue	Mother: Place of birth	Mother: Mother tongue	Whether able to speak English	Occupation: Trade, profession	Occupation: Industry, business	Employer, salary or wage worker	Line
English	Russia	Russian	Russia	Russian	yes				51
English	Russia	Russian	Russia	Russian	yes				52
Romania	Romania	Romania	Romania	Romanian	yes	Peddler		OA	53
Romania	Romania	Romania	Romania	Romanian	yes	None			54
Romanian	Romania	Romanian	Romania	Romanian	yes	worker	factory	W	55
Romanian	Romania	Romanian	Romania	Romanian	yes	Conductor	Railroad	W	56
Romanian	Romania	Romanian	Romania	Romanian	yes	Salesman	office	W	57
Romanian	Romania	Romanian	Romania	Romanian	yes	worker	office	W	58
Romanian	Romania	Romanian	Romania	Romanian	yes	Clerk	office	W	59
Austrian	Austria	Austrian	Austria	Austrian	yes	Tailor	store	OA	60
Hungarian	Hungary	Hungarian	Hungary	Hungarian	yes	Painter	bldg	W	61
Russian	Russia	Russian	Russia	Russian	yes	Lawyer	office	OA	62
English	Hungary	Hungarian	Hungary	Hungarian	yes	None			63
English	Russia	Russian	New York	English					64
Austrian	Austria	Austrian	Austria	Austrian	yes	Salesman	firm	W	65
Austrian	Austria	Austrian	Austria	Austrian	yes	None			66
Austrian	Austria	Austrian	Austria	Austrian	yes				67
Austrian	Austria	Austrian	Austria	Austrian	yes				68
Austrian	Austria	Austrian	Austria	Russian	yes	officer	bank	W	69
English	Russia	Russian	Russia	Hungarian	yes	None			70
Hungarian	Hungary	Hungarian	Hungary	Hungarian	yes	None			71
English	New York	English	Hungary	Hungarian	yes				72
English	New York	English	Hungary	Hungarian	yes				73
English	New York	English	Hungary	Hungarian	yes				74
English	New York	English	Hungary	Hungarian					75
Romanian	Romania	Romanian	Romania	Romanian	no	None			76
Romanian	Romania	Romanian	Romania	Romanian	yes	operator	shop	W	77
Romanian	Romania	Romanian	Romania	Romanian	yes	Painter	shop	W	78
Russian	Russia	Russian	Russia	Russian	yes	Painter	House	W	79
Russian	Russia	Russian	Russia	Russian	yes	None			80
English	Russia	Russian	Russia	Russian	yes				81
Russian	Russia	Russian	Russia	Russian	yes	dressmaker	shop	W	82
Austrian	Austria	Austrian	Austria	Austrian	yes	None			83
Austrian	Austria	Austrian	Austria	Austrian	yes	Stenographer	office	W	84
English	Austria	Austrian	Austria	Austrian	yes	Stenographer	office	W	85
English	Austria	Austrian	Austria	Austrian	yes	Clerk	office	W	86
English	Austria	Austrian	Austria	Austrian	yes	None			87
Austrian	Austria	Austrian	Austria	Austrian	yes	Dressmaker	shop	OA	88
Russian	Austria	Austrian	Austria	Austrian	yes	None			89
Austrian	Austria	Austrian	Austria	Austrian	no	None			90

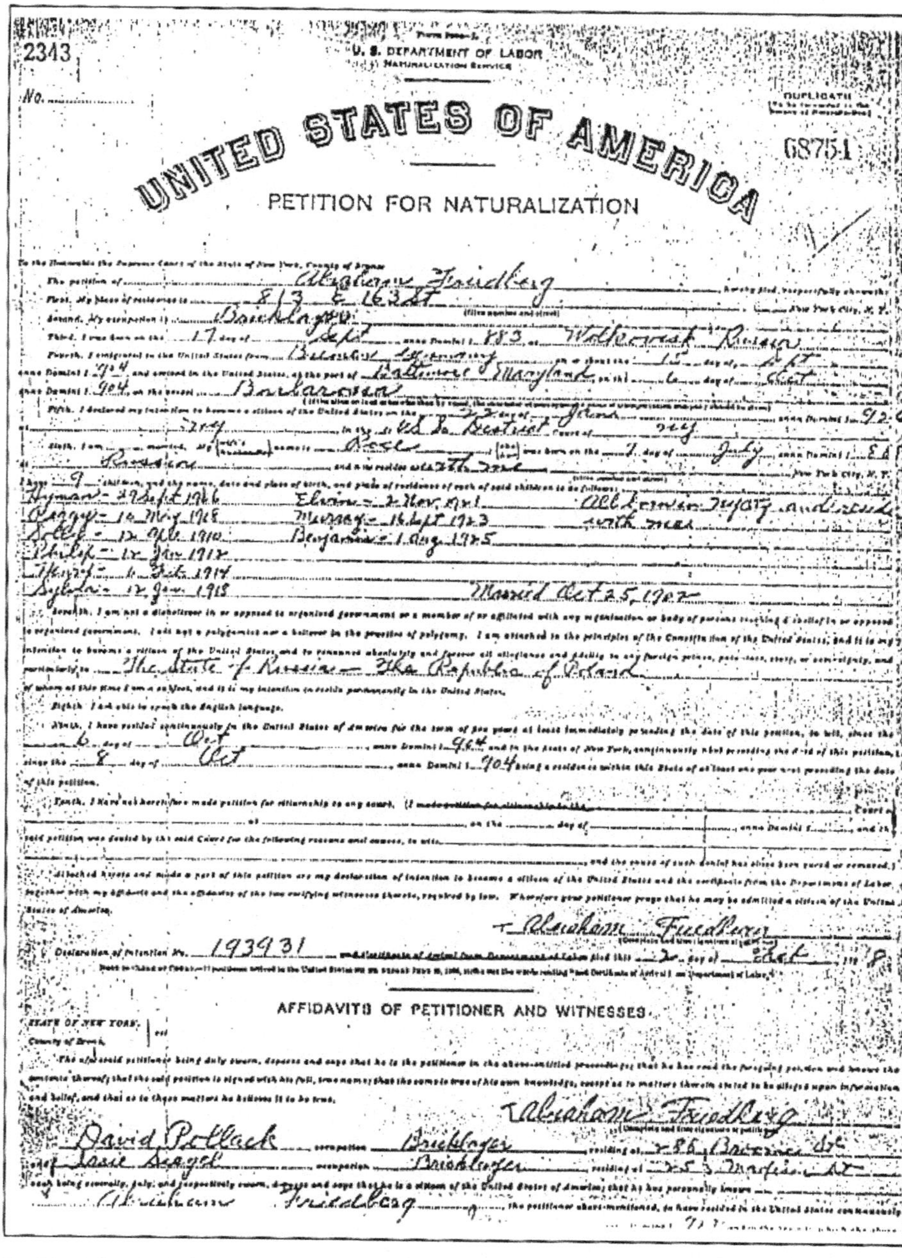

2343

U. S. DEPARTMENT OF LABOR
NATURALIZATION SERVICE

No. ....

DUPLICATE

68751

UNITED STATES OF AMERICA

PETITION FOR NATURALIZATION

AFFIDAVITS OF PETITIONER AND WITNESSES

Petition for Naturalization: The "Final Papers" filled out before being granted citizenship contains a wealth of information about the applicant and family including the birth dates and places of the applicant, his wife, and children. It shows the applicant's marriage date, home address, occupation, date of arrival, and the ship on which the applicant arrived.

Tombstone Inscription: *The Hebrew inscription on a Jewish tombstone allows you to go back one additional generation, because it gives the name of the father of the deceased. This picture identifies three generations of Tartaskys. Shown is Manny Tartasky at the grave of his father, Me'er Tartasky, who the inscription says is the son of Yechazkel Tartasky. The inscription states Me'er died on the seventh day of Passover, 5659. Using the calendar converter tool at JewishGen.org, this converts to April 1, 1899.*

YAD-VASHEM
P.O.B. 84 Jerusalem, Israel

Martyrs' and Heroes' Memorial Authority
DAF-ED
For the registration of the victims of the disaster.

רשות הזכרון לשואה ולגבורה
דף־עד
לרישום חללי השואה

יד ושם

Registr. No. .... מס. הרישום

Photo תמונה

חוק זכרון השואה והגבורה — יד ושם תשי"ג 1953
קובע בסעיף מס' 2
תפקידו של "יד ושם" הוא לאסוף אל המולדת את זכרם של כל אלה מבני העם היהודי, שנפלו ומסרו את נפשם, נלחמו ומרדו באויב הנאצי ובעוזריו, ולהציב שם וזכר להם, לקהילות, לארגונים ולמוסדות שנחרבו בגלל השתייכותם לעם היהודי.
(ספר החוקים מס' 132 י"ז אלול תשי"ג (28.8.1953))

The Martyrs' and Heroes' Remembrance (Yad Vashem) Law, 5713-1953 determines in Art. No. 2 that
The task of Yad Va-Shem is to gather in to the homeland material regarding all those members of the Jewish people who laid down their lives, who fought and rebelled against the Nazi enemy and his collaborators, and to perpetuate their memory and that of the communities, organizations and institutions which were destroyed because they were Jewish.

Surname	SITTNER פרל / סיטנר	1. שם המשפחה
First name	Regina née PERL [רגינה]	2. השם הפרטי
Name of Father	Joseph PERL	3. שם האב
Name of Mother		4. שם האם
Date of birth	1871	5. תאריך הלידה
Place and country of birth	BEUTHEN Germany	6. מקום וארץ הלידה
Permanent residence	Germany	7. מקום המגורים הקבוע
Occupation	Housewife	8. המקצוע
Nationality before German occupation	German	9. הנתינות לפני הכבוש הנאצי
Places of residence during the war	Holland	10. מקומות המגורים במלחמה
Place, date and circumstances of death	Westerbork to Auschwitz	11. מקום המות, הזמן והנסיבות
Family status: Bachelor/Married/Number of children	married	12. מצב משפחתי רוק / נשוי / מספר הילדים
Name of wife and maiden name/Age	—	13. שם האשה ושם משפחתה לפני הנשואין / גילה
Name of Husband/Age	PAUL SITTNER	שם הבעל / גילו

Place and date of death המקום והזמן שנספו	Age הגיל	14. שמות הילדים עד גיל 18 שנספו (מעל לגיל זה רושמים ב"דף־עד" מיוחד) Names of deceased children up to the age of 18 (over the age of 18 fill out another form)
Westerbork to Auschwitz May 1944	73	

Note: Children must be registered on the form of one of the parents only.
הערה: את הילדים יש לרשום ב"דף־העד" של אחד ההורים אך לא יותר מפעם אחת.

I, the undersigned Gerhard SITTNER אני
Resident at (full address) P.O.BOX 6642 Johannesburg South Africa הגר ב (כתובת מלאה)
Relative/Acquaintance of Son קרוב/ה מכר/ה של

Hereby declare that the details of my testimony are true and correct to the best of my knowledge and belief.
מצהיר/ה בזה כי העדות שמסרתי כאן על פרטיה היא נכונה ואמיתית, לפי מיטב ידיעתי והכרתי.

Signature G. Sittner חתימה Place and date Jerusalem 27. May 1968 מקום ותאריך

Signature of Office Clerk .... חתימת הפוקד

Page of Testimony. *More than 3 million Pages of Testimony at Yad Vashem document Holocaust victims providing information about the victim and the name, address and relationship of the person submitting the document.*

LISTE DE DÉCÉDÉS DE BERGEN-BELSEN APRÈS LA LIBÉRATION

(FEMMES).

NOMS ET PRÉNOMS.	DOMICILE.	DATE de naissance	LIEU DE NAISSANCE.	[illegible] de [illegible]
AUSSEL Marguerite				16. [illegible]
BARON Gisèle	Chenu (Sarthe)	9. 7.07	CHENU	6. [illegible]
BAUDRY Yvonne	Toulouse	26. 4.22		10. [illegible]
BENNAROS Anette	Paris	16. 2.20		25. [illegible]
BERGER Bella				[illegible]
BERRIER Jeanne ou Janine	Vic-le-Comte	17. 7.01		30. [illegible]
COUSSON ou GOUSSON Honorine.	Quincey (Vienne)	20.12.95		fin [illegible]
DARQUES Alice	Pas-de-Calais	12. 5.02		31. [illegible]
DUBOIS Yvonne		10. 2.17	AUTUN	4 [illegible]
FREIBERG Sala				22. [illegible]
FRENID Madeleine				19. [illegible]
GELBSKY Marie				7. [illegible]
GOGEAU Françoise				11. [illegible]
GOLDBERG Rose		20. 4.18	GRENOBLE	27. [illegible]
GOLDENBERG Annie	Paris	18. 2.95		21. [illegible]
GULLIANO Henriette				15. [illegible]
HAUTIER Marie	Bregnac (Dordogne)	21.12.02		3. 6. [illegible]
HIBON Prudence	Nord	7.10.95		? [illegible]
JORDAN Ida	Juan-les-Pins	8. 4.12		28. [illegible]
LACHOT Marie-Louise	Côte-d'Or	10.10.99		17. [illegible]
LEBLANC Geneviève	Aubusson	5. 6.08		5. [illegible]
MARCHILE Muguette				7. [illegible]
MARTIN Gabrielle	Lyon-Bretteau	19. 6.04		8. [illegible]
MASERAUX Françoise				[illegible]
MATTAU ou MAZEAU Jeanne.	Dordogne	11. 3.24		6. 6. [illegible]
MIRIVOL Marie				6. [illegible]
MOKOTOVICZ Rebecca	46, rue des Marais, Paris	1.12.23	May 22 1944	25. [illegible]
NOURRY (Dr) Anne-Marie	15, rue Émile-Duclaux, Paris.			9. [illegible]
NUSSBAUM Elisabeth				5. [illegible]
PAYEN Léa	Dury	21. 6.99		20. [illegible]
PHILIPPE Yvonne	Nîmes	7. 3.05		10. [illegible]
PITOIS Louise	Ille-et-Vilaine	20.10.04		[illegible]
POLIN Hélène		30 ans		[illegible]

Holocaust Document: *List of persons who died in Bergen Belsen concentration camp after the liberation of the camp includes the name of Rebecca Mokotowicz. She was deported to Auschwitz from Paris on May 22, 1944.*[9] *She survived a death march to Bergen Belsen but died on May 29, 1945, at the age of 21,*[10] *34 days after the camp was liberated. She is buried in a grave at Bergen Belsen.*[11]

---

9 *Memorial to the Jews Deported from France 1942–1944.* Serge Klarsfeld. New York: Beate Klarsfeld Foundation, 1983.

10 Above document part of Yad Vashem collection.

11 Documentation in the possession of the International Tracing Service, Bad Arolsen, Germany.

Index Cards of the International Tracing Service

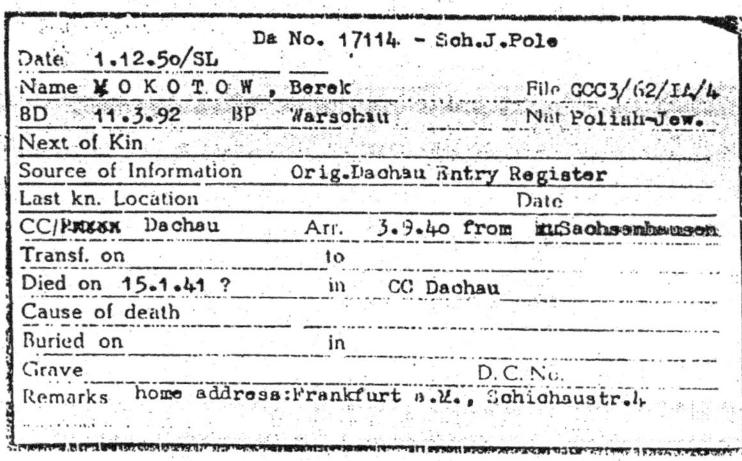

Da No. 17114 - Sch.J.Pole
Date 1.12.5o/SL
Name MOKOTOW, Berek File GCC3/62/IA/4
BD 11.3.92 BP Warschau Nat Polish-Jew.
Next of Kin
Source of Information Orig.Dachau Entry Register
Last kn. Location Date
CC/Prison Dachau Arr. 3.9.40 from Sachsenhausen
Transf. on to
Died on 15.1.41 ? in CC Dachau
Cause of death
Buried on in
Grave D.C. No.
Remarks home address:Frankfurt a.M., Schichaustr.4

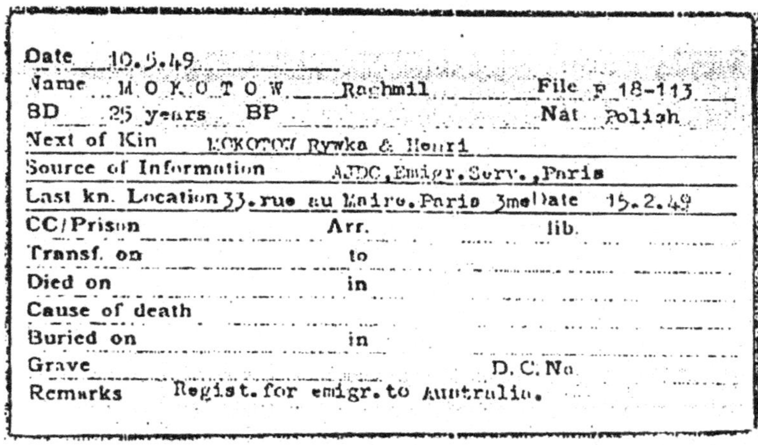

Date 10.5.49
Name MOKOTOW Rachmil File F 18-113
BD 25 years BP Nat Polish
Next of Kin MOKOTOW Rywka & Henri
Source of Information AJDC,Emigr.Serv.,Paris
Last kn. Location 33.rue au Maire.Paris 3me Date 15.2.49
CC/Prison Arr. lib.
Transf. on to
Died on in
Cause of death
Buried on in
Grave D.C. No
Remarks Regist.for emigr.to Australia.

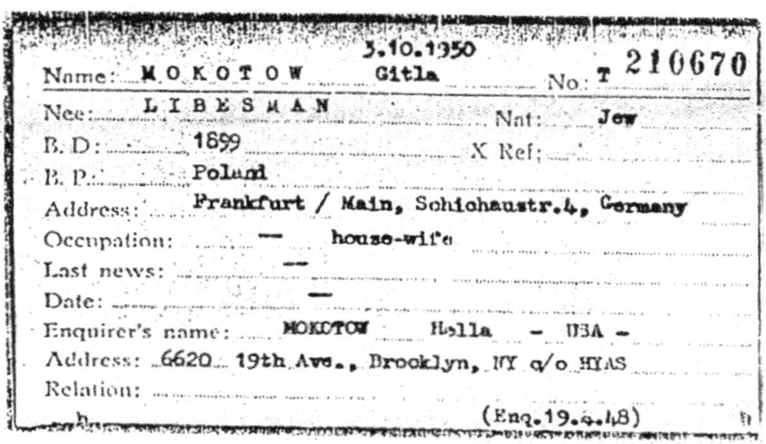

3.10.1950
Name: MOKOTOW Gitla No: T 210670
Nee: LIBESMAN Nat: Jew
B.D: 1899 X Ref:
B.P.: Poland
Address: Frankfurt / Main, Schichaustr.4, Germany
Occupation: — house-wife
Last news: —
Date: —
Enquirer's name: MOKOTOW Hella - USA -
Address: 6620 19th Ave., Brooklyn, NY c/o HIAS
Relation:
(Enq.19.4.48)

Index Cards of the International Tracing Service. The International Tracing Service in Bad Arolsen, Germany, has information on more than 17 million people persecuted by the Nazis that place the person in a certain place at a certain time. It is one of the major Holocaust collections in the world.

(Top) Index card for a Holocaust victim.

(Middle) Index card for Holocaust survivor.

(Bottom) Index card that is an inquiry as to the fate of a person caught up in the Holocaust

```
~~~~~~~~~~~~~~~~~~~~~~~~~~~~~~~~~~~~~~~~~~~~~~~~~~~~~~~~~~~~~~~~~~~~~~
JEWISHGEN Digest for Sunday, March 14, 2010.

1. New feature on Greater Tel-Aviv burial society site
2. Re: A retroactive name change?
3. Reply to:  a retroactive name change
4. Do you recognize Morris ROSENFELD?
5. RABINOWITZ, Belarus-->New York-->Kansas City
6. need help re family tree program
7. Re: Minneapolis Jewish Cemeteries
8. Is Porabka Uszewska, Poland near Tarnow?
9. Re: Reply to:  a retroactive name change
10. Request for Translation of Marriage Record Written in Russian
11. Hebrew/Yiddish gravestone translations needed
12. BERNER brothers to St. Louis from Chernigov (Chernihiv) Ukraine

----------------------------------------------------------------------

Subject: New feature on Greater Tel-Aviv burial society site
From: Israel P
Date: Sun, 14 Mar 2010 14:23:32 +0200
X-Message-Number: 1

The website of the burial society of Greater Tel-Aviv -
http://www.kadisha.biz/ - has added a new feature. (I'm not sure when - I
just saw it this morning.)

When you look at the grave site, they tell you who is buried on either
side.  Those are live links, so you can easily click through them to find
the names at the ends of the rows.

You cannot do a lookup based solely on location, but this is a very good
alternative.

Israel Pickholtz
Jerusalem
----------------------------------------------------------------------

Subject: Re: A retroactive name change?
From: Paul Silverstone
Date: Sun, 14 Mar 2010 11:38:49 -0400
X-Message-Number: 2

I have seen the same thing - changing the surname of the parent in
Poland - on applications to the US govt, such as for Social Security.
The deceased father who never left Poland was given the new American
surname of the applicant.  I think it just made everything a little easier.
Paul Silverstone

Peter Lebensold wrote:
> Shelley asked:
>
> "The second question concerns the surname Barnett. When Hyman Barnett
> remarried he gave his (deceased) father's name as Hyman Barnett.  Would
> I be correct in assuming that these were both anglicised names and that
> Hyman would have been Chaim?  And that Barnett was often given to jews
> with various "B" names on entering England?"
```

JewishGen Discussion Group. *Sample of the postings to the JewishGen Discussion Group. At the top is a summary of the 12 postings and below it the detail of the first two postings.*

JewishGen Family Finder
preserving our history for future generations

JewishGen Family Finder

Run on Wednesday 1 September 1999 at 14:20:09

JewishGen's latest and most ambitious project involves traveling to your ancestral shtetl and documenting and preserving what you find there. Click here for more information on the 1999 programs.

Searching for Surname FINKELSTEIN

Number of hits: 140

This search request has been made possible through the *JewishGen-erosity* of
The JGS of Greater Washington in memory of Sheiala Moskow

Surname	Town	Country	Last Updated	Researcher (JGFF Code)
Finkelstein	Tirgu Neamt	Romania	Before 1997	Arye Barkai (#1020) [redacted]
Finkelstein	Vaslui	Romania	Before 1997	
Finkelstein	Ivano Frankovsk	Ukraine	Before 1997	Nina C.R. Henry Price (#1042) [redacted]
Finkelstein	Lviv	Ukraine	Before 1997	
Finkelstein	Marijampole	Lithuania	Before 1997	Michael Reynolds (#1064) [redacted]
Finkelstein	Slavantai	Lithuania	Before 1997	
Finkelstein	Iasi	Romania	Before 1997	Gary Papush (#1191) [redacted]
Finkelstein	Pamoitz	Lithuania	Before 1997	Richard Orkin (#1300) [redacted]
Finkelstein	Pittsburgh, PA	USA	Before 1997	Delaine Winkler Shane (#1371) [redacted]

JewishGen Family Finder: *Internet database containing the names of ancestral towns and surnames being researched by more than 85,000 genealogists worldwide. Shown here is the beginning of the list of persons researching the surname Finkelstein.*

Avotaynu Soundex Search Result

The Data Bases column shows the codes for the various databases in which the surname appears. Scroll the screen down below the list of surnames to see the "List of Databases and Number of Surname Entries in CJSI". For each database, there is its code, followed by a brief description. This description has a link to a more detailed description of the database. Follow the link to learn how to access the database. Some databases are on-line, others are in books or microfiche.

Soundex	Name	Data Bases
765843	BANGELSDORF	B
765843	BENGELSDORF	ABCDGMZ
765843	BENGELSDORFF	P
765843	BENGIELSDORF	E
765843	FANKELSHTEJN	D
765843	FEINKELSTEIN	K
765843	FIENKELSTEIN	A
765843	FINCHELSTEIN	IK
765843	FINCKELSTEIN	CP
765843	FINKEELSTEIN	A
765843	FINKELCHTAIN	K
765843	FINKELSHTEIN	BCGZ
765843	FINKELSHTEJN	D
765843	FINKELSHTERN	D
765843	FINKELSHTOK	D
765843	FINKELSTEI	A
765843	FINKELSTEIN	ABCFGIJKLMNOPQTVYab
765843	FINKELSTEINAITI	K
765843	FINKELSTEINAS	I
765843	FINKELSTEINS	I
765843	FINKELSTEJN	CK
765843	FINKELSTINE	A
765843	FINKELSTON	A
765843	FINKELSTSEIN	P
765843	FINKELSZTAIN	L
765843	FINKELSZTEIN	KL
765843	FINKELSZTEJN	IK
765843	FINKIELSTAJN	K
765843	FINKIELSTEIN	IK
765843	FINKIELSTEJN	JK

[Show previous 30 records] [Show original 30 records] [Show next 30 records]

Enter a Surname for a new Search: [ ] Search Clear

List of Databases and Number of Surname Entries in CJSI

Visit our Home Page for more information about Avotaynu

- A. AJGS Cemetery Project Burials (51,453 surnames). 400,000 Jewish burials in various locations throughout the world.
- B. JewishGen Family Finder (28,411 surnames). Surnames being researched by some 12,000 Jewish genealogists worldwide.

Consolidated Jewish Surname Index: Internet database which provides sources of information for more than 700,000 Jewish surnames. Shown are sources for the surname Finkelstein (and spelling variants). The column headed Data Bases contains codes for each of the databases included in the project whose descriptions are shown below the list of surnames.

SOCIAL SECURITY Death Index

SSDI @ RootsWeb

Social Security Death Index Search Results

August 1999 Update - 61,964,627 records - Updated Monthly

The most full-featured and up-to-date SSDI search engine on the internet

Field	Value	Records	Results
Last Name	FINKELSTEIN	2485	2485
First Name	ABRAHAM	34155	45

Results 1 thru 15 of 45

Next

Name	Birth	Death	Last Residence	Last Benefit	SSN	Issued	Tools
ABRAHAM FINKELSTEIN	20 Sep 1897	Dec 1978	02116 (Boston, Suffolk, MA)	02146 (Brookline, Norfolk, MA)	018-14-0173	Massachusetts	SS-5 Letter Add Post-em
ABRAHAM FINKELSTEIN	28 Dec 1884	Oct 1971	02131 (Roslindale, Suffolk, MA)	(none specified)	030-16-2221	Massachusetts	SS-5 Letter Add Post-em
ABRAHAM FINKELSTEIN	15 Feb 1907	Jul 1979	90035 (Los Angeles, Los Angeles, CA)	90035 (Los Angeles, Los Angeles, CA)	034-24-9732	Massachusetts	SS-5 Letter Add Post-em
ABRAHAM FINKELSTEIN	12 Jun 1910	May 1982	11572 (Oceanside, Nassau, NY)	11572 (Oceanside, Nassau, NY)	050-01-0537	New York	SS-5 Letter Add Post-em
ABRAHAM FINKELSTEIN	24 Apr 1885	Oct 1968	11214 (Brooklyn, Kings, NY)	(none specified)	050-05-3936	New York	SS-5 Letter Add Post-em
ABRAHAM FINKELSTEIN	21 Mar 1911	Feb 1978	10016 (New York, New York, NY)	(none specified)	050-18-1374	New York	SS-5 Letter Add Post-em

Social Security Death Index: *Internet database containing the names of some 90 million people for whom there was a Social Security death benefit claim starting in 1962. This illustrates a number of men named Abraham Finkelstein who appear in the database.*
Source: Rootsweb.com.

CPSIA information can be obtained
at www.ICGtesting.com
Printed in the USA
BVOW04s0348241216
471798BV00003B/4/P

9 780983 697596